SECRET OF THE LOST COLONY

BY

REBECCA PRICE

JANNEY

Multnomah Publishers • Sisters, Oregon

SECRET OF THE LOST COLONY
published by Multnomah Fiction
a division of Multnomah Publishers, Inc.

© 1997 by Rebecca Price Janney
International Standard Book Number: 1-57673-018-2

Cover illustration by Tony Meers
Design by D² DesignWorks
Printed in the United States of America

For information:
MULTNOMAH PUBLISHERS, INC.
POST OFFICE BOX 1720
SISTERS, OREGON 97759

Library of Congress Cataloging-in-Publication Data:
Janney, Rebecca Price, 1957-
    Secret of the Lost Colony/by Rebecca Price Janney.   p. cm.   (The impossible dreamers series; bk. 1) Summary: Lindsey, Andrew, and Ben travel back in time with their home-school teacher to the English colony on Roanoke Island, where the people are struggling to survive an unfriendly environment and a problem of low supplies.   ISBN 1-57673-018-2 (alk. paper)   [1. Time travel–Fiction. 2. Roanoke Colony (N.C.)–Fiction. 3. Roanoke Island (N.C.)–History–Fiction.] I. Title. II. Series: Janney, Rebecca Price, 1957- Impossible dreamers series; bk. 1.
PZ7.J2433Sh   1997   97-15998
[Fic]–dc 21   ·   CIP   AC

97 98 99 00 01 02 03 — 10 9 8 7 6 5 4 3 2 1

To my favorite teachers:
Roberta Haas
Phil Rohm
Robert Weiner
Earl Pope
David Willis
Samuel Hugh Moffett

ACKNOWLEDGEMENTS

In my search for the Lost Colony I had enthusiastic assistance from three employees at Fort Raleigh National Historic Site: Ranger John A. Gillikin, Jen Richards, and Jill McDaniel. I also appreciate Michael Moore's lesson in Elizabethan dress and attitudes. (Michael portrayed one of the queen's soldiers in "The Lost Colony" theatrical production at FRNHS. My notes tell me you get an A, Michael!)

I am also grateful to Bill Barker, the Thomas Jefferson interpreter at Colonial Williamsburg. Bill's remarkable performances inspired me to use President Jefferson in the overall concept of *The Impossible Dreamers*. Bill is one of many wonderful people who make Williamsburg very special to me.

In addition, thanks to Richard James of the Schuylkill Center for Environmental Studies in Philadelphia for his expert information about hurricanes.

Finally, while no one knows exactly how the Lost Colony mystery actually played out, the conclusion Lindsey Skillman and her "impossible dreamers" reach is based on extensive research and is quite possible.

Chapter One

I think it's so neat how T.J. talks about history like he's right there." Thirteen-year-old Lindsey Skillman shoveled her Wheaties into her mouth as she spoke. Her parents would not have approved, but they had left for work.

"It creeps me out," Ben Tyler remarked as he chewed his hot buttered toast. Steam from his hot chocolate fogged his wire-rimmed glasses, and he pushed them up on his nose.

"Well, I like how he gets that faraway look in his green eyes," Lindsey said dreamily, "and suddenly he's in another world."

"Oh, puh-leeze," her brother Andrew groaned. "I think you're in another world. You're always mooning over T.J., making goo-goo eyes at him. He's not so great."

Lindsey had first met T.J. when the youthful teacher began leading her Sunday-school class at church. Her parents and aunt had been discussing home schooling ever since their cousin Ben had come to live with them after his father's death two years earlier. But they were too busy: Dr. Skillman was a philosophy professor at the College of William and Mary, Mrs. Skillman worked as a court reporter, and Mrs. Tyler traveled a lot with the Richmond Symphony Orchestra. When Lindsey told them about T.J. and how he had lost his job, her parents and Aunt Mary Ann hired him to home school Lindsey,

Andrew, and Ben. Now T.J. lived in an apartment in the Skillmans' basement.

Lindsey and Ben had done well so far under T.J.'s tutelage, but her eleven-year-old brother was another story. So far, not so good.

Lindsey opened her mouth now to defend herself, but just then T.J. walked into the kitchen. Her face went scarlet, and she ducked behind the cereal box. She wished the baseball player pictured on the front would pull her inside. Andrew's back was turned to the teacher, though, and he kept right on going.

"T.J. this and T.J. that. I'm sick of hearing his name." He snorted. "And what a name!"

Lindsey elbowed Andrew to make him stop, but her brother simply ignored her. "Thomas Jefferson Wakesnoris! Whoever heard of a name like that!" His blue green eyes danced mischievously as he laughed and banged on the table, sending a spoon clattering to the floor. "Of course, the name fits. The way he falls asleep! Man, how does he do that? At the drop of a hockey puck he's off in la-la land."

"A-hem." The tall, red-haired tutor cleared his throat. "I believe this belongs to you."

He handed the spoon to Andew, who grew even redder than Lindsey knew she must be at the moment.

"It's time for class," T.J. said calmly.

He never had to yell or get sarcastic. Wakesnoris simply stared, and his students fell into line. Although he had a bear of a last name and was unusually sleepy, he was so dignified you couldn't write him off as a geek or a nerd. Lindsey certainly couldn't. Besides, he was a direct descendant of President Thomas Jefferson.

Abandoning her over-ripe banana—a treat Lindsey loved—she jumped up from the table, grabbed her books, and rushed past T.J. down the hall to their classroom. Their house was a hundred years old and had plenty of space. A parlor on the first floor had become their home school. Ben and Andrew hurried closely behind her and plunked themselves into their seats.

T.J. entered the room then, sat at the edge of his desk, and began swinging his long legs like he always did. He moved around a lot, probably to keep himself awake. Lindsey's father had told them that T.J. once taught at Williamsburg High School but that he kept falling asleep, so he was fired. Dr. Skillman had done a little research and discovered that, while the teacher was brilliant, he had a big problem—a disease called narcolepsy. He would suddenly fall asleep no matter where he was. That's why he could no longer teach in a regular school, his supervirsors had decided.

"Let's begin with prayer," T.J. announced now. "Lord, we thank you for this beautiful day and ask that all we learn might be to your glory and for our good. In Jesus' name, amen."

"Amen," Lindsey and Ben echoed.

Andrew would usually roll his eyes at this point, but he must have known he was already in enough trouble. "Amen," he muttered.

After the pledge of allegiance and a Scripture lesson, T.J. rolled a metal lectern toward him and put his notes and history text on it. "Open to chapter three, please."

Lindsey snapped her book open, as did Ben. Andrew had apparently forgotten his. T.J. looked first at Andrew, then at the empty space in front of Lindsey's brother.

"I...I, uh, I left it in my room," he stuttered.

"Go get it. Quickly."

"Yes, sir."

"Oh, brother." Lindsey sighed. When was he going to grow up, anyway?

Less than a minute later, Andrew was back in his seat, thumbing his way to chapter three.

"I'm going to ask y'all some questions about the Lost Colony," T.J. said in his soft Virginia accent. "Who sent the first English ships to explore the outer banks of North Carolina?"

"Sir Walter Raleigh." Lindsey was eager to regain his approval.

"Correct. What year did that happen?"

"1584." Ben beat her to the punch.

"Why did they go?"

"To establish a fur trade and get gold and silver." Lindsey smiled sweetly at Ben. He responded by pushing his glasses back into place; they constantly slid down his nose.

"Uh-huh. And when the explorers reported back to England, they told Raleigh how perfect the place was for a colony. Is that true?"

"No," Ben spoke quickly. "The soil wasn't any good, and storms pounded the ships. There wasn't any gold or silver either."

T.J. nodded. "Very good."

"I have a question." Lindsey didn't bother to raise her hand. "Why didn't Sir Walter Raleigh go there himself?"

"Well, Queen Elizabeth liked him a lot. She didn't want him going on dangerous journeys."

"Were they in love?" she asked, then blushed at how stupid

she sounded. Andrew and Ben burst into giggles.

"Some say they were." T.J. smiled. "Okay, when did the first colonists arrive on Roanoke Island?"

"Uh, 1587," Ben guessed.

"Close. There were actually two groups. The first consisted of 108 men. They arrived in 1585 and had a hard time of it. They took seven ships, and the main one was almost lost in a storm." As he spoke, the teacher became animated. "The inlet was so shallow that only the smallest ships could get through. The others anchored a few miles out to sea, but they got pounded there. Most of the food supply was lost in the water."

Lindsey watched T.J. closely as he explained how the first colonists depended on Croatoan Indians for food and protection from hostile tribes. His face glowed with excitement, and he gestured with his long, artistic hands. She found herself swept up in the drama of the adventure.

"When a colonist lost a silver cup, he charged an Indian with stealing it," T.J. went on. "For revenge the English burned the Indian's village, killing many women and children. When the next group of colonists arrived in 1587, the Croatoans were understandably nervous. What tragic thing happened?"

No one knew. Lindsey riffled through her book for the answer, but once again, Ben was faster.

"A colonist got shot full of arrows when he was out crabbing."

Lindsey shivered as she pictured the scene.

"That's right. But the Englishmen stayed. They lived in simple houses built just outside a small earthen fort. The first group had built the fort."

"Wasn't a little baby born there, too?" Lindsey asked.

"Yes. The first English child born in North America was the granddaughter of Governor John White. He was in charge of the colony and a fine artist who drew many pictures of Native Americans and their habitat. Andrew, can you tell us what his grandchild's name was?"

He shook his head sullenly.

"Virginia Dare," Lindsey blurted.

"Yes." T.J. looked at Andrew, who squirmed under his gaze. "Things looked pretty bad for the colonists. They arrived in July, too late to plant crops. The Croatoan Indians were the only ones who could help them when the food ran out. A colonist had accidentally killed a Croatoan, though.

"Manteo had gone to England and liked the colonists. He was a Native American who tried to bring the two groups together. Finally, the colonists ended up sending Governor White back to England for supplies. But he didn't come back when he had promised."

T.J. stared at something far beyond them, beyond the room itself. It was like he could see in some magic mirror those events that had happened long ago. Lindsey wondered if he was about to fall asleep. She poked her cousin's fleshy arm, and they nodded at each other.

They all waited, and then T.J. twitched, waking himself up. "In 1588 the Spanish attacked England," he said as if nothing had happened. "It took every ship England had to pull off a victory. Governor White repeatedly begged Queen Elizabeth to let him return to the Roanoke colonists." He shook his head sadly. "But she couldn't afford to lose even one or two ships."

T.J. started staring again and didn't say anything for a full minute. The boys snickered, which startled the teacher. "In 1591

White returned to Roanoke, beside himself to see his family again. As his ship drew closer to the island, he saw smoke rising from the settlement. But when he got ashore, no one was there."

"No one?" Andrew was shocked; he obviously hadn't read the story.

"No one."

"But why was there smoke?" Lindsey asked.

"Probably lightning—no fires had been lit for a long time."

"Where did they go?" Ben asked.

T.J. spoke slowly and stared, like he was in a trance. "No one knows."

"What happened to them?" Lindsey raised her voice to get his attention.

At first he just kept shaking his head and mouthing, "No one knows." Then he stopped.

"I think he's asleep," Ben whispered.

Andrew snickered.

"I think so, too. Maybe we'd better wake him up." Lindsey walked over to T.J., whose eyes were now closed. His breathing was deep and slow. Putting her hand on his shoulder, she shook him. "Wake up, T.J." Nothing. "C'mon, T.J." She nudged him harder.

Then a strange thing happened. Lindsey tried to pull her hand away, but she couldn't. It felt glued to T.J.'s arm.

"Ben!" she cried. "My hand is stuck!"

Ben rushed to her side and yanked at her hand. "I can't get it off," he wailed after several tries. "Oh, no!" He stared at his own arm. "Now I'm stuck to you!"

"C'mon, you guys," Andrew jeered. "Quit messing around."

"We're not joking!" Lindsey screamed. A strange feeling began to fill her body. It rose upward from the tips of her toes and was now at her knees.

"What is that?" Ben looked around wildly.

"Do you feel it, too?" Lindsey asked.

Frowning, Andrew rose and tried to pull Ben away from Lindsey, and Lindsey away from T.J. But then Lindsey felt a fierce undertow sucking her down, down, down. It felt like she was caught in a rip tide at the shore.

"What's going on!" she yelled, but then everything grew dark.

Chapter Two

O h, my hand, " Lindsey moaned as she rolled over on a hard, flat bed. She began to rub her right hand, but when she raised her left hand to see what was wrong, she saw only a blur. She blinked hard to clear her foggy vision. She felt like she was climbing out of the deep well of a dream. Something was definitely wrong. She sat up with a start—and banged her head on the wooden bunk bed above her.

"Ouch!" Without thinking, she tried steadying her dizzy self with her sore hand. "Oh—ow!"

Andrew and Ben, who were lying on the upper bunk, didn't stir. Her cousin's raspy snores filled the darkened room. Now she understood why they called snoring sawing wood.

A noise at the glassless window caught Lindsey's attention. A leather shade covered the opening, and it gently banged against the window. Pieces of daylight filtered into the room. Lindsey heard people talking outside. She couldn't tell what they were saying, though. She glanced at her hand.

"It seems okay," she said aloud and shook it gently. Maybe she had just slept on it. But then she realized she hadn't been sleeping at all. "I was in school, and I wasn't wearing this awful outfit."

Lindsey examined the pale blue dress that cascaded over her like a tent. It was made of a coarse cottonlike fiber. She knew it would set off her aqua-colored eyes, but there was no mirror anywhere in the room she could look into. A white cap lay on her bunk.

"I don't think we're in Williamsburg," she muttered softly. She got up and wandered around the crude, one-room hut. A rustic table stood to the left of the sleeping area. Clean, heavy-looking utensils and pewter dishes lay on top of it. Two small benches flanked its longer sides. A homemade broom stood in a corner by the door, where cape-like coats hung from pegs.

A wood fire gently burned in the fireplace. Lindsey promptly sneezed from the sharp fragrance of smoldering pine. There were other odors as well: musty, clinging ones like mold and wet beach towels that had laid around for too many days. "I don't think this is even my century," she said with a sense of awe.

She glanced about, wondering what had happened to T.J. Excitement pulsed through her like ice water. She decided she'd better wake up the guys. "Oh, gu-u-ys," she called musically, "wake u-u-p."

"No-o-o," her brother whined, flopping from his side onto his stomach. "Oof!" He was no more used to that hard bed than she was.

Ben was a grumpy waker, too. "Go away, Lindsey!"

"C'mon!" she shouted. "Something amazing has happened."

"Can't you let a guy sleep?" Andrew said sharply.

"This isn't sleep."

"I'll get you for this. If you think—" He stopped. "What...?" Andrew sat up slowly, taking in the strange room and his clothes.

He and Ben sported dark wool pants that ended in a snug band just below their knees. Saggy white stockings covered the rest of their legs. They wore sleeveless vests of faded brown leather over long-sleeved white shirts.

"Whoa, what's this?"

"Will you shut up?" The normally gentle Ben got snippy when he was rudely awakened. He shoved Andrew, then howled. "My hand!"

Andrew pushed right back, then winced. "My hand is sore, too. Hey, Lindsey, what's goin' on?"

"I don't know. When I woke up, here we were. For what it's worth, my hand hurts, too, and I'm thirsty." Lindsey leaned against the mud and timber wall and folded her arms across her chest.

Ben tried to push up his glasses in his customary way, but they weren't there. "My glasses...I thought I had them on." He looked around him. "Things are a little blurry. Where are we, anyway?"

"I don't know yet, but don't everyone go nuts." Lindsey tried to calm them down. She was, after all, the oldest.

"Toto," Ben said, referring to Dorothy's dog in *The Wizard of Oz,* "I don't think we're in Kansas anymore."

"That's for sure!" Lindsey exclaimed. "I think something wonderful has happened."

But her cousin didn't seem to think it was so great. "Could we be dreaming this?" He and Andrew hopped off the bunk bed.

"Impossible," she replied. "If I don't like a dream, I can always wake myself up. This time I can't."

"What's with our hands?" Andrew asked testily.

"It must have happened when we were grabbing each other's arms," Lindsey explained.

Ben snapped his fingers. "It's all coming back." He looked around the dim room. "Hey, where's T.J.?"

"The jerk," Andrew said hotly. "I'm going to get him fired."

"He is not a jerk!" Lindsey stamped her foot.

"Oh, no? Then why are we in this mess? That guy's a weirdo."

"Man, it's hot!" Ben pulled his collar away from his neck. "Why are we in these stupid clothes? What's going on?"

Lindsey paced the dirt floor. From beyond the dreary one-room house, she could hear voices and the pounding of hammers.

"Look at those ceiling beams." Ben pointed above his head. "I've never seen any like that before."

Andrew stared at the leather shades that covered the windows. "This place looks really old-fashioned."

"So do our clothes," Ben said. "I wonder where we are."

"Or *when* we are," Lindsey countered.

"If it weren't so crazy, I'd say we're back in time." Ben laughed nervously. "But it is crazy. Let's get out of here before whoever lives here gets back. That would be scary. We'd be in so much trouble—"

"Guess what?" Andrew shouted. "We already are in trouble—big trouble!"

"Are you going to act up or grow up, little brother?" Lindsey's eyes flashed.

Andrew stuck his tongue out at her.

"C'mon, you guys," Ben pleaded. "We don't have time to argue."

"Okay," Andrew agreed. "Let's just get out of this place. Lindsey, you go first."

"Follow me!" Lindsey was eager to find out what was going on.

The boys stood right behind her as she carefully pushed the knobless door open to the outside. "Everything does look old-fashioned," she said as they stepped into the light of a very humid day.

"How old-fashioned?" Ben's voice trembled.

"Hundreds and hundreds of years." She could hardly believe this was happening.

Lindsey blinked rapidly in the bright sunlight. A warm breeze blew around them as they stood close to the hut-like house. Her pulse raced as she imagined what would happen when someone finally noticed they were there. But no one paid much attention to the trio. The frowning people in costumes like theirs went on their merry—or in this case grumpy—way in a real hurry.

In this strange neighborhood small homes with thatched roofs bordered a narrow dirt road. Suddenly a few men who were building newer versions of the same houses stopped working. Everyone pushed past Lindsey and the boys toward an earthen fort at the end of the dirt road.

"Stupid chicken!" Ben suddenly shouted, kicking at a bird that was pecking at his clunky leather shoes.

"Hey!" someone yelled. "That's my chicken!"

A boy about their age ran toward them, his face red with heat and anger. "Were you trying to steal my chicken?"

"N-no," Ben stammered. "It attacked me."

"A likely story! Just remember, fool, this one's mine." He shoved Ben in the chest and made off with the squawking fowl.

"Creep! I wasn't going to take his stupid old chicken. What a grouch."

"It's no wonder in this awful heat," Andrew said.

"We'd better be careful what we do after that little episode," Lindsey warned.

"My, aren't we smart using big words?" her brother said mockingly.

"I wonder who these people are and what's upsetting them," Ben asked quickly. He always tried to stay out of Lindsey and Andrew's squabbles.

Lindsey slapped at a mosquito that was dining on her right ankle. "Man, that hurt!"

"What hurt?" But before she could answer, Ben was slapping at the back of his neck.

All around them men, women, and children talked rapidly as they hastened toward the earthen fort. Just then a cruel-looking man stopped another man and warned, "Do not cross me at that meeting today, John."

"You do not threaten me," the other said calmly.

"We shall see." The first man sniffed and stormed off.

"Do you think we're in frontier days?" Ben asked the others. "I can't see as well as I'd like."

Andrew frowned. "I don't think so. I think we would see calvary if this were back then."

"That's *cavalry,*" Lindsey corrected.

"Okay, know-it-all!" Andrew's hands were at his hips. "Where are we then?" He was sensitive about being dyslexic, which made him confuse the order of letters and numbers.

"If I didn't know better, I'd say this was the 1580s," Lindsey said dramatically.

Ben slapped his palm against his forehead. "Say! Do you think this might be the Lost Colony?"

"I think it might—"

"Are you coming or not?" A small girl about Lindsey's age stood before them. Her blonde hair was coarse from lack of washing, and she smelled sour from layers of unwashed sweat.

"Uh, I, uh..." Lindsey backed away. "Coming where?"

The girl rolled her expressive eyes. "To chapel. All adults are supposed to be there daily, Lindsey. How could you forget?"

"I, uh, I have been feeling a little weird today."

"I should say so, if you could forget something like that! Hurry up!" she coaxed. "I will save you a place." With that she took off.

Lindsey, Ben, and Andrew gaped after her.

"How did she know your name?" Ben asked.

"I have no idea." Lindsey shook her head in disbelief. "We'd better go to chapel, though. I guess it's that building inside the fort. Maybe we'll find out more there."

"That's just great!" Andrew exclaimed. "I could be centuries from home, and I still have to go to church!"

Lindsey and her family had gone to church, not daily, but every Sunday for as long as she could remember. When she was seven, she had asked Jesus into her heart. Maybe at chapel God would give her a sense of what was happening here, and she could tell the boys. Andrew might scoff to think that God had anything to do with all this, but there had to be some explanation.

They started to follow the mysterious girl when they heard a familiar voice drifting slowly and calmly on the humid wind. "Hey, y'all!" They turned as one to see T.J. Wakesnoris, who wore the same period clothes as the guys.

"T.J.!" Lindsey threw herself at the tutor like a lost child who had just found her parent. Although she was excited

about the possibility of an adventure, she felt better knowing
T.J. was nearby. She backed away now, noticing how the old-
fashioned clothes made him look more handsome than ever.
On the boys they just seemed ridiculous.

"I had no idea." T.J. shook his head. All around them,
people rushed to chapel.

"No idea about what?" Lindsey asked.

"Do you know where we are?" Andrew looked as if he
might want to throw their teacher to the wolves.

The teacher nodded. "Roanoke Island."

"The Lost Colony?" Andrew's eyes nearly bugged out.

"The very one."

Lindsey clapped her hands. "That's terrific! But how did we
get here?"

T.J. took her by the arm. "Let's get away from this crowd."

They all followed him to the edge of the fort closest to
Roanoke Sound, the waters of which they could hear clearly.
Once they were alone the tutor said, "I had no idea I could take
anyone with me."

"What does that mean?" Lindsey wrinkled her eyebrows.

T.J. mopped his forehead with a linen handkerchief, then
returned it to his pocket. "You know how I fall asleep?" They
all nodded. "Well, once something strange happened to me
after I was studying a mystery that caught my attention. I fell
asleep thinking about it, and I…"

"What?" Lindsey pumped. "What?" The idea of time traveling had always fascinated her.

"I found myself at the very place I was thinking of."

No one spoke for a few moments.

"Like back in time?" Lindsey asked.

"Yes."

"How could you?" Ben said. "That's not possible."

"Oh, but it is. Just never like this."

"What's that supposed to mean?" Andrew demanded.

"I've never gone back with anyone." He paused. "Do y'all remember what happened right before you got here?"

"You were talking about the Lost Colony, and then you went into a trance," Lindsey explained. "You fell asleep, and I tried to wake you up, but my hand stuck to your shoulder."

"Yeah, and I tried to pull her away, but I stuck to her," Ben added. "Then Andrew got sucked in, too. Our hands really hurt where we held on to you."

"That's very strange." T.J. pulled at his chin.

"It's okay, though, right? You got back before when this happened." Ben picked nervously at his vest.

"Ye-s-s." T.J. sounded uncertain.

"But you've never had to take three people back either."

"So, fall asleep again, will you, and let's get out of here," Andrew yelled.

"I'm afraid it doesn't work that way." The teacher shook his head. "When it happened before, the mystery had to resolve itself first. Also, I didn't fall asleep like I normally do until close to the time when I found out what had happened."

"When are we going to get home then?" Andrew demanded.

T.J. looked him in the eye. "I haven't a clue."

Chapter Three

Lindsey watched as a strand of reddish blond hair slipped over T.J.'s eyes. He brushed it back with his left hand, and Lindsey sighed. Everything he did affected her that way.

She tuned back in to the conversation. "When you went back before, how long did you stay?"

"That's hard to explain, Lindsey." T.J. became thoughtful. "Have you ever read a book or seen a movie about time travel?"

"Sure. I've always been fascinated by it."

"You know how when the characters return, it's like they never left? No one even missed them?" Lindsey and the boys nodded. "It's like that."

"What if someone tries to talk to you while you're gone?" Lindsey asked. "Could the people back home tell you weren't there?"

T.J. shook his head. "I don't know. As I told you, it only happened once before. Plus, I was alone. By the way, how are your hands?"

All three checked and agreed that their hands felt much better.

"And to think I never liked history," Andrew said.

"This is a great adventure." Lindsey smacked her arm. "If it weren't for these blasted mosquitoes!"

"It is an adventure," T.J. agreed.

Suddenly someone interrupted them. "Thomas! Is that you?"

A tall man in his early twenties approached them. Lindsey recognized him as the man named John who had been threatened a little earlier. He wore an odd-looking helmet shaped like a triangular bucket. Underneath it his sandy-colored hair swung at his shoulders, and he wore a beard. His eyes reminded Lindsey of an Irish setter's, kind and steady. Like the girl they'd just met, he smelled like he hadn't bathed in a long time; his scent was like wet leather.

T.J. greeted the man with a hearty handclasp, as if he'd always known him. "It's me, all right."

"This pleases me greatly." John noticed Lindsey then and respectfully removed his helmet. "Hello, Lindsey."

She wasn't sure what to do, and so she curtsied awkwardly.

"Hello." He nodded toward the boys as if he knew them too, then turned back to T.J. "This could get tense today," he said in a hushed tone as if conveying a secret.

"Yes, I can see that," T.J. agreed politely.

"What about you? What do you think should happen now that the savages have failed to meet us?"

Lindsey bristled at the word "savages." What a rude way to refer to Native Americans! She watched to see how T.J. would respond.

"I'm still pondering the matter," he said.

This seemed to satisfy John. "I think you are a good man, Thomas Wakesnoris. I can count on you. Father Martyn said so."

The teacher bowed. "Thank you."

"I see that at least your children are thriving in our colony," John said, changing the subject.

Lindsey's eyes nearly popped out. He thought T.J. was their father! She couldn't bring herself to look at Ben or Andrew for fear they would all burst out laughing.

T.J. didn't miss a beat. "Yes, we are all well, thank you."

"Except for these lousy mosquitoes," Andrew muttered. By this time each of them had several bites.

"It is a shame we have so little food on which to live." John shook his head sadly. "We must correct that problem. As for the pests, I think some mud mixed with water will comfort your bites, Andrew. If the swelling worsens, you may see Dr. Newton for his calamine treatment." He paused, then said, "Well, I shall see you momentarily at chapel." He grinned sweetly at Lindsey as he left.

"Your children?" Andrew sputtered.

"Shhh!" T.J. cautioned. "Apparently that's what you are here. We'd better get to chapel," he said and began to walk at a fast pace.

"Do you think we'll really find out what happened to the lost colonists?" Lindsey asked breathlessly, trying to keep up with her teacher's long strides.

"I do."

"That is so cool, T.J."

"You know," he said thoughtfully, "maybe you'd better call me 'Father' here."

Lindsey frowned. That was too strange. Still, she spoke for all of them when she said, "In this case, calling you 'Father' is probably the best thing to do." She thought for a moment. "We met this girl right before we saw you, and she knew us. She even called me by name like that man did just now. Was it that way when you time traveled before?"

"Yes," he said. "I fit right into the action. People know me. I'm part of their community."

"But do you know who *they* are?" she asked, swatting another mosquito. This part could get old pretty fast.

"Only the famous ones. Y'all need to pay really close attention to what's happening so you can blend in."

"How do people know us?" Andrew asked with a frown. "We didn't even exist back then."

"I don't know," T.J. said as he smashed a mosquito on his arm.

"Do you have any say in what happens to history?" Lindsey asked. They were nearing the simple wooden chapel now.

"I'm afraid not. I can only see the results." T.J. looked sad about this.

"Well, that's stupid," Andrew said. "If we have to be here, there must be something we can do."

T.J. stopped so suddenly in his tracks that Ben bumped into him with an "Ugh!" Ben bounced off and turned red with embarrassment. "No, there is nothing you can do. Just forget that idea."

"Well, I just meant…"

"Do you understand me?"

"Yes, sir," Andrew yielded under their tutor's piercing stare.

"That goes for y'all." T.J. looked at Ben, then at Lindsey.

"That's fine, sure," they chorused.

"Now, we'll stick together at chapel. And the less y'all say, the better."

"No problem," Ben said. "They talk so funny here anyway. They're so formal."

"You know this chapel thing?" Lindsey said. "That girl said adults have to go every day—I think she meant that we're adults." She shook her head. "I don't get it."

"In this culture the three of you are just entering adulthood. In fact, y'all would be married in a year or two." T.J. smiled at their shocked faces. Lindsey actually rather liked the idea, but her brother clearly did not.

"That's gross!" he shouted.

"Look, little brother, like it or not, you're a grown-up here. So act like one!"

"As your father, I command you to stop this," T.J. said with a twinkle in his eyes.

At the center of the fort they entered the chapel's dark sacredness. T.J. removed his hat respectfully. Up at the front of the chapel on a beautifully carved altar lay an enormous Bible, with candles burning on either side. Although the hundred or so people made it warm and musty, Lindsey felt cooler without the sun beating down on her. She also was grateful that the mosquitoes hadn't followed them inside. They took their seats on roughly hewn benches toward the back.

"There you are!" The girl they had seen earlier shoved her way past T.J., Andrew, and Ben and sat down next to Lindsey. Lindsey, who sometimes took two or three showers a day during the summer, felt overwhelmed by the girl's tart smell. She tried to move away, but there wasn't enough room on the bench.

"I asked Mother and Father if I could sit with you, and they said yes." The girl leaned over toward T.J. "How are you, Mr. Wakesnoris?"

"Fine," he said.

"Well, are you not going to greet me?" the talkative girl asked the boys.

"Hi," they said lamely. Andrew wrinkled his nose. Lindsey glared at him, and he turned back to the front.

Lindsey heard low voices coming from all over the chapel.

They sounded like an orchestra when it warms up.

"There could be quite a fight today," the girl whispered in Lindsey's ear. "You know how nervous everyone is."

"You mean about supplies?" Lindsey remembered from her textbook that supplies were a big problem for the colonists.

She nodded. "That, too. Isn't it dreadful how little food we have? That foolish Captain Fernandes spent so much time privateering that we used up most of our food. And this soil! I do not understand how anything can grow in it!"

Lindsey was glad she had read her assignments. She recalled that Governor White had had a hard time getting the fleet's captain to drop them off as promised. She decided to take a small risk.

"Are you unhappy that we landed here instead of the Chesapeake?" she asked.

"You must believe it!" the girl exclaimed in a hushed whisper. "Governor White is terribly angry with Captain Fernandes. We all are. And now we are going hungry. The good captain does not care, though." She crossed her thin arms across her chest. "Father has not gone crabbing, and that has further reduced our food stores. Mama will not budge, though. She would rather be a little hungry than a widow."

"You mean since the Indian shot that guy through with arrows?" Lindsey asked excitedly.

The girl's face flushed in anger. "Lindsey, how could you? That was Uncle George."

"I...I'm sorry," Lindsey stammered. "Sometimes I'm in another world."

"Well, that is all right. Father keeps saying lightning never strikes twice in the same place. Still, Mother will not let him leave the settlement. Not even to seek revenge against the savages."

There was that word again! She didn't think she liked this girl.

Just then another young lady passed behind them and tapped Lindsey's companion on the back. "Hello, Bess Payne!"

This was helpful. Now, at least Lindsey could call the girl by her first name, as if she knew her.

Then chapel began. A dark-haired, bearded priest named Father Martyn led the congregation in the daily morning prayer and Scripture reading. Until then Lindsey hadn't even realized what time of the day it was. The brief service was a little odd to her ears with its "Oh ye's," "Praise ye's," and "Bless Thy's." But when the priest read from Psalm 139, the words brought Lindsey to tears. "Where can I go from Thy Spirit?" Father Martyn read aloud. "Or where can I flee from Thy presence? If I take the wings of the dawn, If I dwell in the remotest part of the sea, Even there Thy hand will lead me, And Thy right hand will lay hold of me." That God was near in this hundreds-of-years-ago time meant a lot to her. Time traveling might be thrilling, but it did present its dangers. She felt comforted by the familiar psalm. She may not know *why* she was there, but at least she knew she wasn't alone. God was watching over them.

After the service, Father Martyn made an announcement. "Governor White has requested that his assistants remain behind." Then he gave the benediction, and everyone else filed out of the building into the potent heat and humidity.

Before leaving, Lindsey caught a glimpse of the colony's governor. A well-dressed man of medium height and build,

John White had light brown hair and a beard speckled with gray. He wore an elegant black coat with gold stripes, a white ruffled collar, and a fancy sword at his side.

"Thomas!" John, the man who had stopped T.J. earlier, pulled him aside. "I desire to speak with you later. Where may I find you?"

T.J. didn't answer right away. Lindsey watched him. He was probably wondering where a young family man would go after morning worship at "the Cittie of Raleigh," as the colonists called their settlement. Another man intercepted them at that moment, however, and asked if T.J. would help with the day's fishing while Ben and Andrew helped unload the boats.

"Of course," T.J. replied, then turned back to John. "Will you join us for dinner this evening?"

"Yes, thank you," he said. "Please pray for us and our decision."

Lindsey started to ask what she should do when Bess came over.

"Come," Bess said. "Mistresses Dare and Harvie require us."

Not knowing what lay before them, the "impossible dreamers" went to their tasks.

Chapter Four

I never felt so stiff in my whole life!" Andrew complained loudly as he stretched out on his bunk bed. "I'm definitely going to have T.J. fired when we get back."

"There's not even a decent pillow!" Ben moaned. "This flat thing is pathetic. I don't even know what's in it."

"You guys think *you* worked hard today," Lindsey said. She wished she had her own room, away from the boys. At least she had her own bed.

"What could you have done that was as hard as lugging barrels and crates from the ships to the island?" Andrew asked.

"That does sound hard," Lindsey admitted.

"It was," Ben spoke up. "I'm not used to that kind of work. My neck and back ache."

"Are you all done?" Lindsey asked.

"I wish," Andrew said. "The men running the show told us we have at least a few more days worth of this."

"I think that Captain Fernandes guy who brought everyone to Roanoke Island may be even more upset than us," Ben said.

"He wants out of this dump," Andrew added. "So do his crew and those boys who worked with us today."

"Not Thomas Archard. He's trying to make the most of it."

"That wimp!" Andrew spat. "Well, George Howe sure hates this place."

Lindsey was confused. "The guy who was killed crabbing?"

"No, his son," Andrew said. "He'd do anything to leave. I wish he would go and take me with him! As soon as we get back—*if* we get back—that weirdo of a teacher is getting the boot."

"I wish you wouldn't say *if* we get back," Ben complained.

"And I wish you wouldn't hang around with that Howe kid, Andrew," Lindsey said. "He's trouble."

"Yeah, well, this place is trouble, so they go hand in hand," Andrew returned.

Although Lindsey still thought of this as an adventure, she didn't much care for the hard labor or the terrible housing. In addition, her sensitive skin was bruised from at least twelve mosquito bites. She fought the urge to scratch them; she knew they could get infected that way. Her willpower wasn't always up to the challenge, however. She sure wished she knew what God was up to, bringing them all here.

"What did you do today, Lindsey?" Ben asked.

"Well, first that girl Bess and I made lunch for the two women expecting babies," she said, grateful for her cousin's interest.

"You mean that smelly kid?" Andrew wrinkled his nose.

Lindsey rolled her eyes. "Then we unpacked their barrels and arranged their household things."

"That doesn't sound too bad. Why are you so tired?" Lindsey knew Ben wasn't trying to pick a fight, but his question irritated her.

"You try cooking oatmeal in a cast iron pot over an open flame!" she answered in an annoyed tone. "I almost caught my clothes on fire from standing too close. And the whole time there's this really pushy woman hanging over me with breath like rotten hamburger. She kept telling me everything I was doing wrong."

"Who was she?" Ben asked.

"Her name's Agnes Wood." Lindsey sighed. "She's ancient and the biggest busybody I ever met! Imagine how excited I was to be making Virginia Dare's mother's lunch! That doesn't happen every day, you know. But poor Mrs. Dare didn't get a word in edgewise. Agnes kept butting in, complaining and ordering me around. Besides all that, she's missing a bunch of teeth and looks like a carved pumpkin. Ooh, I felt like screaming."

"You're doing a pretty good job of it now," Andrew smirked.

"Just what I need, little brother. A nice kind word."

"But I thought this was an adventure," he mimicked. He hated being called "little brother." That's why she did it.

"You don't understand!" Lindsey wailed. "It is. I'm glad to be seeing all this stuff, but..." She hesitated. "Everyone's so dirty, and it's so hot. Then there are these lousy mosquito bites." She started scratching again. "Our history books never talked about how dirty and miserable it was back then."

Ben became thoughtful. "Like Williamsburg. In the historic area everything's so quaint. But if you lived in colonial times, it was horse pies everywhere."

"Hello!" T.J. entered the house then, and all three children started talking at once about where they'd been and what they'd seen. He walked over to their bunks and listened patiently until they had run out of words.

"I don't think we need to ask what you did." Lindsey frowned at the fish smell all over him.

"Yeah, you stink!"

"Andrew!" Ben gasped.

"Well, he does. Did you go fishing or what?"

T.J. smiled sheepishly. "Yes, with Father Martyn, and I'm afraid I do smell. But at least I brought dinner." He motioned toward the kitchen area. "Speaking of which, we'd better get moving since we have a guest dining with us tonight."

"That man from church?" Lindsey asked.

"Uh-huh. John Wyles. Y'all should call him Master Wyles, though. He's one of Governor White's assistants. Oh, and don't forget to call me Father."

"That'll be tough, but I'll try," Ben said.

Andrew sighed. "Why can't you just fall asleep and take us home where I already have a father?"

"Andrew, I am sorry about getting you into this," T.J. said. "However, I'm still your guardian, and you must respect my authority."

No one said anything for a minute.

"I think we'd better take showers before we fix dinner," Lindsey said, finally breaking the silence. "So..." She started looking around. "Where is it?"

"What?" T.J. asked.

"The shower."

"Uh, Lindsey, there are no such things in the sixteenth century on Roanoke Island."

"Oh, of course!" She slapped her forehead with her right palm. "They must've only had bathtubs back then."

"Wrong again."

"What do you mean?" Lindsey stared at him.

"There are no bathrooms here," he explained. "These people

didn't bathe. They thought it wasn't healthy."

"You're kidding!" they all said in unison.

"Sorry, but it's true."

"So that's why everyone around here stinks to high heaven," Andrew said.

T.J. laughed.

"So we just have to put up with it?" Lindsey asked.

"Sorry," her teacher said.

"This is the pits!" Andrew nearly choked on his own words. "When are you going to get us home?"

"Just as soon as I figure out how to," T.J. said, then narrowed his eyes. "Until then, Andrew, I suggest you use a more polite tone. It also wouldn't hurt you to make the most of the situation."

"Yeah, Andrew," Lindsey said, "you may get to solve a mystery that no one else ever has."

But Andrew continued to sulk.

"So, what are we having for dinner besides fish?" Ben asked too cheerfully.

"Well, now, that's one question I can answer." T.J. smiled. "Who wants to help?"

"I will!" Lindsey shouted. It meant more work, but at least she'd be close to T.J.

"Me, too!" her cousin offered. Both of them hopped off the bunk beds and landed on the floor with a thud.

"I'd like to stay here, sir," Andrew said. "I'm pretty tired."

Lindsey was glad to see her brother was at least trying to remember his manners.

"That's fine. Lindsey and Ben can assist. You can help clean up afterward."

Ben helped T.J. get the fire in the hearth started. Lindsey eyed the fish on the table. Beside them lay some wild onions, yams, and nuts. As red and gold sparks snapped and rose up the chimney, she asked, "What kind of fish are these, T.J.?"

"Trout." He shook his head. "It's not a lot for five people."

"Don't worry, I won't eat much." Lindsey hated eating food if it looked like it had been alive once. She even refused lunch meats if they had the slightest hint of pink in them. And if she cut into a piece of chicken and saw a vein, she lost her appetite.

"We also have corn, which we need to pound and boil so we can make cakes," T.J. said. "Ben, that's a good job for a strong young man like you. I'll show you how to do it in a minute."

"That's it?" Lindsey asked. "That's what these people ate?"

"Yes, Lindsey," T.J. said quietly.

She shook her head. "So much for my sense of adventure."

"I know it's a bit of a shock, but I have a feeling you'll make the most of it," he said. "C'mon, let's get going."

In spite of the trout's sharp odor and the biting taste of the wild onions, dinner wasn't half as bad as Lindsey had feared. The little corncakes and mashed yams actually tasted smooth and sweet. John Wyles certainly enjoyed it all.

"That was a wonderful meal," he repeated for the third time. He got up from the table and stretched. "I know this place has strange food, but at least it is fresh. Oh, those terrible days on the ship enduring sea biscuits and stale water."

Lindsey was glad T.J. hadn't brought them on the ship.

"Miss Wakesnoris, I do enjoy your hearth." He bowed before taking his place once again at the table.

Lindsey's mouth fell open when he called her "Miss Wakesnoris." Andrew blew his nose loudly, and she knew he was trying to cover up his laughter.

"It is good that you have maintained your high spirits," Wyles said. "As you know, things were not so affable at the meeting this day."

"Yes, I heard," the teacher said. "I have not told my, uh, children yet, though."

"My wishes were not heeded," Wyles said sadly. "I know we gave the savages a week to gather for a council so that we could discuss our differences. I know they failed to come together. But I do not believe, as some of Governor White's other assistants do, that the Indians are plotting war against us. News travels much slower here than in England. We do not enjoy the modern conveniences of English life."

Lindsey stifled a laugh—to think John Wyles believed he came from a modern place! When T.J.'s eyes bored into hers, she sobered up.

Ben tried to bring the subject back to the meeting earlier that day. "What did you decide, uh, Master Wyles?"

"I encouraged reason and patience. So did the governor." Wyles shook his head. "The more forceful approach won the day, however. Governor White was compelled to take it."

"What does that mean?" Ben asked.

"Most of Governor White's assistants are troubled. You see, the Indians attacked several men that Lord Grenville left behind last year," Wyles explained. "Those who survived fled south to Croatoan. We do not know what has become of them.

The more forceful among us believe that this, added to Master Howe's death as he went crabbing and the savages' failure to confer with us, means we should attack. Otherwise, they say we shall not be able to live here peacefully."

"Seems just the opposite to me," Lindsey said. "Won't you just make everything worse if you fight them?"

"We will find out, will we not?" the governor's assistant asked glumly. Then he added, "I knew some of Grenville's men, and they provoked the Indians." He sighed heavily. "At any rate, there is to be an attack on Dasmonquepeuc."

"Dasma-who?" Andrew blurted.

"It is a mainland town," Wyles explained. "It is where some think the savages are preparing to strike at us." He looked at T.J.

"I am going to be part of the raid," the teacher told them. "Captain Stafford, who is leading it, needs all of the assistants. Masters Dare and Harvie can't make it, though, because their wives are expecting any day. So I am a substitute." He fell easily into talking like John Wyles.

"Yes, I recommended him," Wyles said.

"Couldn't you recommend someone else?" Ben's face grew pale with fear.

Lindsey knew why. If anything happened to T.J. in the battle, they'd never get back home.

Chapter Five

The first sunbeams filtered through the window the next morning, falling softly on Lindsey's face. She awoke to find herself scratching furiously at every part of her body. At first she thought she was dreaming. In reality, though, her entire body felt crawly and itchy. They would have to do something about those mosquitoes.

Above her Andrew and Ben were squirming, too. A few minutes later her brother vaulted off the bed as if it were on fire.

"What's going on?" he yelled.

"Ew!" Ben shouted. "There are bugs all over me!"

"Bugs!" Lindsey jumped off her bed. "Where did they come from?"

By now all three of them were on their feet, hopping around. Anything to shake off the pests. The rumpus awakened T.J., who had slept on the kitchen table.

"What's going on?" he asked sleepily.

"There are bugs all over us!" Lindsey cried. She had slept in her underclothes, but she didn't feel self-conscious. They covered more of her than some of her outfits back home.

T.J. calmly took the boys outside while Lindsey removed her underclothes and shook them out the window. Then she left the cottage while Ben and Andrew did the same. Afterward, they gathered around the kitchen table while T.J. inspected the bunks. He wanted to find out where the bugs had come from. It didn't take long.

T.J. lifted Ben's pillow. "Here's the problem."

Ben swallowed hard and pushed his glasses up, forgetting he wasn't wearing them.

"It's stuffed with Spanish moss," T.J. said. "Ben, when did you do this?"

"Uh, last night, sir. I had trouble sleeping. The bunk was so hard, and I was really worried about the battle today. So I went outside to look for something soft to stuff my pillow with."

"And you saw the Spanish moss?"

"Well, yeah. The men on the ship yesterday said they used it for pillows and mattresses. They said it's really soft."

"They didn't mention that they process it first." This was more of a statement than a question.

"They process it?" Ben gulped.

T.J. nodded. "Yes, it's soft. Yes, it makes good filler. But it's loaded with tiny bugs. It has to be thoroughly treated before it can be used."

"I'm really sorry." Ben hung his head. "I had no idea. And I couldn't see the bugs in the dark without my glasses, anyway."

"It's okay, son." T.J. clasped his shoulder. "Lindsey, will you start breakfast while the boys and I clean up the bunks?"

"Sure."

"We have to hurry. I'm supposed to leave in half an hour."

Lindsey hated the thought of T.J.'s going with the governor's assistants. She had spent the night dreaming that T.J. got killed in the battle, leaving her and the boys stuck forever in time. Somehow that dented even her adventuresome spirit. She would make the most of it, though.

"T.J.," Ben began, "do you think it's a good idea for you to..."

"How about preparing some corn mush?" T.J. suggested, cutting him off.

"Sure." Lindsey grinned. "But what I'd really like is a bowl of chocolate oat clusters with fresh milk and an over-ripe banana."

The bug-busters shook out the bedding. Then they wiped off the bunks with rags dipped in water from a well near the house. Afterward they gathered at the table. Andrew turned up his nose when he saw the mush. That didn't stop him from digging in, however. T.J. put a hand out to stop him.

"We haven't prayed yet," he said.

Andrew rolled his eyes and plunked down his wooden spoon.

"Lord, we thank you for this food and for your presence with us," T.J. said. "We don't understand exactly how or why we're here. However, we do know that Scripture says whenever two or more are gathered in your name, you are there with them. Please protect our men from harm today, as well as any innocent Indians. Let nothing be done to dishonor you or endanger Lindsey, Ben, or Andrew. You have entrusted them to me. For that reason," and his softly-accented voice cracked, "I ask you to protect me today from evil and bring me back safely. In Jesus' name, amen."

"Amen," Lindsey said, feeling a little comforted by the prayer.

Ben's lips trembled slightly.

"You don't have to pray about this, T.J.!" Andrew shouted. "You just don't have to go!"

"Yes, I do."

"Why?" He crossed his arms defiantly.

"The governor has requested it. A gentleman needs to fulfill his obligations."

"What about your onbligations to us?" Andrew mispronounced the word. Lindsey decided not to correct him this time.

"I'm well aware of them," T.J. said quietly.

"Then don't go. If you die, we'll be stuck here." Andrew was standing now, his body rigid. "You never should have brought us here. You're nothing but trouble! I'm going to have you fired if we ever get back."

"Sit down, Andrew," T.J. said evenly.

Lindsey watched in silence, wondering what her brother would do.

For a moment, Andrew stayed on his feet. But the teacher's gaze must have pierced his hard core. He slowly took his seat.

"I can see how upsetting this is. I apologize for the pain y'all are in," T.J. told them. "I know you're deeply upset, Andrew. And Lindsey, you like the challenge, but you're inconvenienced by the primitive conditions. Ben, I sense your fear. I never would have brought you if I could have helped it. And truthfully, I'm not sure how we'll get back. When this happened before, I just woke up after I discovered how the story ended. I don't understand it, but I know that God made me a certain way. I fall asleep easily, and I'm able to time travel. I also know that God brought us all together. A lot of prayer went into your parents' decision to hire me to teach you. God doesn't make mistakes. We're together for a reason. We're here for a reason. And we have to live here in a way that pleases him, trusting that he'll take care of us and bring us home again."

No one said anything for a long time. Finally, Andrew sat down quietly, and Ben wiped a tear from his eye.

"I would never hurt y'all for anything," T.J. finished.

He got up and moved slowly toward the door, where his hat, cloak, and a leather knapsack hung from pegs. As he put on his hat he said, "Please look after each other while I'm gone. And try to pray for me."

Lindsey jumped up from her chair and hugged him. "Be careful."

"I promise," he said. Then he left.

Lindsey and Ben had just finished cleaning up the breakfast dishes when someone knocked at the door.

"I wonder who that is," Lindsey said.

"It could be George Howe." Andrew moved toward the door.

"I hope not," Ben muttered. "I don't like him."

"I don't either, not after he yelled at you about that dumb chicken," Lindsey said.

But when Andrew opened the door, their caller wasn't Howe. It was a very handsome and friendly-looking young man. Ben introduced him to Lindsey as Thomas Archard and added that Thomas had worked with him and Andrew the day before.

"Hello to you," Thomas said, tipping his hat to them.

She wasn't sure what to do. Then he tossed his blond, curly hair out of his eyes and winked at her. She blushed.

"Come in," Ben said, stepping past Andrew. "What brings you here?"

"I am going to chapel. Will you accompany me?"

They had forgotten all about it!

"Well, count me out," Andrew blurted in his abrupt way.

Lindsey opened her mouth to argue with him, but right then George Howe appeared at the door. He boldly elbowed his way past Thomas, who was about two years older and considerably larger.

"I, too, dislike the sound of chapel," he told Andrew. "How about coming with me instead? We can fish for trout while they are fishing for men." He snorted loudly.

Lindsey glared at him. "I think you are…" But before she could finish, Andrew was shoving past her out the door.

"I'm sorry for Andrew—" Ben began.

"No matter." Thomas Archard raised his hand. "I require no explanation. We all have straying sheep in our families. Mother, Father, and I left ours behind in England." His encouraging smile relaxed Lindsey.

Although the chapel was full again, the morning service did little to soothe Lindsey's fears about T.J.'s safety. For starters, there were a number of somber prayers for Governor White's war party. Then she couldn't quit thinking about Andrew being off with that rogue, George Howe. Adventures could sure get messy.

Following the service Ben and Thomas departed to continue unloading the ships. Lindsey was left to walk home alone. So when she saw Bess walking ahead of her, she quickly caught up. Bess smiled and hooked her arm through Lindsey's.

"Are you ready to tend to the Mistresses Dare and Harvie?" she asked.

"I'm ready." She just hoped that awful Agnes Wood wouldn't

be there again. And she wished Bess wouldn't get quite so close.

As they walked down the dirt road toward the women's cottages, Bess talked about Governor White's military campaign. "Do not trouble yourself, Lindsey," she said. "The Lord will watch over your father."

Lindsey tried to hide her surprise at again hearing T.J. referred to as her dad.

"What I would concern myself about is your brother," Bess added quietly.

"My brother?"

She nodded slowly. "Yes. I have seen him keeping company with my cousin, George Howe. George never has been a boy of a goodly disposition. Since his father was killed, he has become even worse. I fear for him, and for Andrew."

"B-but what can I do?"

"Encourage him to stay clear of George."

"He never listens to me, Bess. We argue all the time. If I told him that, he would do it just to spite me."

"Then I am sorry for him."

"Maybe he would listen to you."

"Perhaps," Bess said slowly, hopefully. "I will see what I can do. You know," she laughed lightly, "you do speak strangely sometimes, Lindsey."

"I do?" Lindsey pointed to herself.

"Yes, but I like you as well as a sister." Bess smiled warmly.

Lindsey enjoyed working around Eleanor Dare and Margery Harvie. It took her mind off T.J. and the risky expedition against hostile tribes. Besides, never in her wildest dreams did she imagine she would someday know Virginia Dare's mother and father! She especially liked the tender way Ananias Dare treated his wife, calling her "Little One" and often applying cool cloths to her flushed forehead. What really blew Lindsey away, though, was how young these couples were. They were just a few years older than herself.

Lindsey sometimes daydreamed about getting married. She saw herself wearing a satin and lace gown with a cathedral train. There would be a Williamsburg Inn reception. Of course, this was all after she graduated from college. Maybe by then T.J. would think she was more than just a cute kid. She laughed to herself. He was really much too old for her, but she couldn't help thinking he was adorable. Well, she wouldn't be ready for ever so long. She guessed they just didn't know any better back then.

Agnes Wood wasn't as much fun to be around as the young couples, but at least handsome and protective Ananias Dare kept her on a short leash. Whenever the old woman started spouting off about their terrible circumstances, Dare would chase her out the door.

"Enough, Mistress Wood!" he would declare. "Tend to Mistress Harvie—and more cheerfully, please."

Agnes would stomp off in a huff, then appear at the Harvies only to repeat her gloomy utterances. That is, until Dyonis Harvie would kick her out of his cottage. Back and forth the men lobbed Agnes Wood like a tennis ball. Lindsey constantly dodged her as she and Bess set up primitive nurseries and took food and water to the expectant mothers. One thing, though—while Agnes fluttered back and forth like a dizzy butterfly, Lindsey had little time to dwell on T.J.'s safety. Every time she did, though, her heart beat faster. And she would pray for his protection.

When Lindsey returned to her own cottage later that day, no one else was there. She removed her soiled white head cap and slumped onto a bench at the kitchen table. "What I wouldn't give for a hot shower, herbal shampoo, and my blow dryer!" she muttered. Her stomach rumbled, too, reminding her of the yucky lunch she'd had—raccoon stew. Lindsey had only nibbled on the corn that was mixed in with the stew. She had tossed the leftovers to some squawking sea gulls, which had so deeply angered Agnes Wood that the woman had swatted Lindsey on the bottom with a broom.

"What are ye doin'!" the woman bellowed as the gulls clattered away.

"I was just feeding them," Lindsey said.

"Well, stop, then!" The woman poked her face two inches away from Lindsey's. Lindsey automatically drew back.

"We cannot waste our victuals on those scavengers, child! Ye should be ashamed of yourself." Agnes Wood put her hands on her substantial hips, her feet astride like a statue.

Now, as Lindsey reflected on the incident, she growled in disgust. "I can't stand that old woman!"

Yet not even the memory of raccoon stew could stop Lindsey's hunger. She rummaged around the kitchen craving her mother's spaghetti but willing to wolf down anything edible. Then she stopped for a moment. Did her parents and aunt even know their children were missing? Probably not. Somehow that made everything worse.

Lindsey found some cornmeal and drew fresh water from

one of several communal wells. Then she lit a fire and cooked corn "bread." Unfortunately it looked more like corn Jell-o. Ben wandered in during this process.

"I'm glad real food is on the way," he said, sitting down on a bench. "You know I like to eat, Lindsey, but this stuff they chow down on makes me sick. It's gross enough to turn me into a vegetarian!"

"I know exactly what you mean." She grinned. "You know, if I remember correctly, the lost colonists had a really bad food shortage."

Her cousin sighed heavily. "Oh, well. Maybe I'll finally drop some tonnage." He patted his stomach.

"Where's Andrew?" Lindsey asked, looking around.

"I haven't seen him since this morning." Ben frowned. "I thought he'd be here."

"Maybe we should go look for him," Lindsey suggested. Where could he be? Where would that George Howe take her brother? If anything happened to him...

"Could we eat first?" Ben asked.

In spite of her concern, Lindsey nodded, and Ben said the blessing. Then they ate quietly, but Lindsey missed T.J. and was worried about Andrew, so she hardly tasted the food.

"I'm not too concerned about T.J.," Lindsey said after swallowing a bite of wet cornbread. "I don't expect him until maybe tomorrow." She could at least try to keep up her cousin's spirits. Then she thought about Andrew again. "Did you see Andrew at all today?"

"Just once. He and George Howe were talking to one of Captain Fernandes's assistants."

"What do you think he's up to?"

"Andrew? I'm not sure, but I'm really getting kind of scared. He hardly talks to me and just laughs if I try to say anything—"

"Oh, why don't you just cool it?" Andrew sputtered as he suddenly entered the cottage.

"Where've you been?" Lindsey demanded. "We've been worried about you."

"Save it, Lindsey. I'm taking care of myself."

"We need to know, Andrew," she said.

"You don't need to know anything," he sneered, and just as abruptly as he'd appeared, he left the house, slamming the door behind him.

"See what I mean?" Ben said.

"What is with him? I don't like this at all. That Bess told me today her cousin George is a troublemaker."

Ben pulled at his hair. "I have to get out of here." He jumped up, knocking over a pitcher of water. Then he fled from the house.

Lindsey understood. It was all too overwhelming—the bugs, aching muscles, fears for T.J., worries about Andrew, and a growing terror that they might never get home.

Chapter Six

"Oh, Ben, I feel totally scuzzy!" Lindsey complained. "I've worn this outfit for three days in a row now." Back home she sometimes switched outfits three times a day if her mood changed.

Ben placed two pewter plates of overly-thick porridge on the table. Lindsey thought he seemed calmer following their long walk the night before. She'd gone after him when he'd run from the house, and they had talked long into the night. Andrew, however, hadn't returned at all. He knew she was already worried over T.J.; he couldn't have picked a worse time to take off. Where was he?

"If it's any comfort, Lindsey, I feel pretty yucky, too." Ben tugged at his leather vest. "I've been working in the sun in this same outfit." He sighed, and his eyes became a little glazed. "What I wouldn't give for a hot shower."

"I'm sorry, Ben. You have it a lot worse than I do."

"Oh, I didn't mean that at all!" he said quickly. "We both have it tough. At least my hair is short." He ran a hand through his light brown hair. "Yours must keep you hot and sticky."

"This is the only time in my life I've wished it were short." She smiled. "But it doesn't bother me too much. It's always under that white cap."

"As I unload the ships, I've been looking for a trunk with our name on it," Ben told her. "Nothing has turned up, though."

"Thanks for trying. It would be nice to have at least one change of clothes."

They sat down at the table, and Lindsey apologized for the appearance of the food. "It's not like my mom's oatmeal, that's for sure."

"No, but I'm hungry, and well, it's not raccoon stew, anyway." Ben half-smiled.

Lindsey made a few poor attempts at cheerful conversation. But she couldn't stop thinking about Andrew, and she was mighty worried about T.J. Hanging between them like a delicate web was the awful fact that if anything happened to T.J., they probably wouldn't get home.

Someone knocked at the door just as they were about to leave for chapel.

"Maybe it's Bess," Lindsey said.

Ben's brown eyes twinkled. "My guess is it's Thomas Archard."

"You guys are getting to be good friends. He seems really nice."

"I think he wants to be your friend, too," Ben said.

"You're kidding, right?" In her mind's eye, though, Lindsey pictured fourteen-year-old Thomas's curly hair, hazel eyes, and hint of a beard. She swung open the door and there he was, all right. "Hello, Thomas. Please come in." She was trying to talk like the lost colonists, with more formality and fewer contractions. She often forgot, though, and got stared at for it.

"Good morning, Miss Wakesnoris." Thomas tipped his hat to them as Lindsey fought not to giggle over her new identity—or the handsome Thomas's earnestness. "May I accompany you to chapel?"

"Yes, of course," Ben said.

"Uh, Thomas, you may call me Lindsey, you know."

He seemed startled but pleased by her offer. "Lindsey it is, then."

As they headed off to chapel, Thomas asked about Andrew.

"He went somewhere with George Howe last night," Ben told him. "He hasn't come back."

"Oh, that is grave." Thomas shook his head.

"Why?" Lindsey cried as she stopped and turned to him. Several chapel-goers stared at her.

"Do forgive me for upsetting you, Miss Wakesnoris, uh, Lindsey," Thomas said. "I simply meant that Andrew is not in the best company. George Howe never has been known for his good judgment. Since the tragic death of his father, he has become more reckless."

"So I've heard," she muttered as they continued walking.

"What should we do?" Ben spread his hands in a helpless gesture.

"We must pray for Andrew to come to his senses. We may also be on the look-out for him as we work today."

"Do we have more unloading to do?" Ben asked wearily.

"Yes. I do believe this is the last of it, though."

"Will you also be looking out for our trunks, in addition to my brother?" Lindsey asked. "We seem to be missing them."

"We have very little in the way of clothes or goods," Ben explained.

"Indeed, yes," Thomas said earnestly. "It grieves me to find you so burdened."

Lindsey almost giggled at his way of speaking.

After chapel the young men went to work. Lindsey and

Bess met each other on their way to help the Dares and Harvies. Lindsey was finding it easier to be around Bess; she was even growing to like her. She found herself mentioning her lack of clothes to her new friend now.

At first Bess didn't respond. Then she paused and faced Lindsey. "Dear Lindsey, you must allow me to help you." She cheerfully sized her up. "We are roughly the same size. Both of us are delicate. You may borrow a dress from me."

"I may?" Lindsey cried. "Thank you ever so much!"

"We have some time before Mistress Wood begins to bark orders at us," Bess tittered. "Let us go to my cottage and change you."

Fifteen minutes later Lindsey felt like a new person. Bess had given her a clean outfit from her family's trunk. The pale yellow frock wasn't much to look at, but at least it was clean.

"You know, Bess," she said, "I hate wearing this over an unwashed body. Give me a few minutes, and I'll join you at work."

The girl frowned. "All right," she agreed, obviously not understanding Lindsey's obsession with cleanliness.

Lindsey hurried back to the Wakesnoris cottage, where she took a pail of unused well water into the bunk area and started washing herself with an old cloth. Fortunately she also had a sliver of soap they used for the dishes. She just had to accept that there was no running water with which to rinse. She felt ten times better when she finished washing, even though she hated the thought of wearing that ugly dress. When she heard someone at the outer door, she quickly dried and dressed herself. She rounded the corner of the bunk area, and there was T.J.

"T.J.!" She threw her arms around the dirty, obviously fatigued teacher. Then she nearly bit her tongue. Father Martyn stood just behind him.

"T.J., is it?" The bearded priest smiled. "Is this a pet name?"

"Uh, yes," Lindsey said quickly. "Yes, it is."

The tutor breathed a sigh of relief, though not very heavily. Lindsey noticed that he walked stiffly, and his normally ruddy complexion was the color of skim milk.

"Are you hurt?" she asked as Father Martyn helped the tall man onto a bench.

"Yes, Lindsey," he said, trying to smile. "But I am all right."

"Are you—is everyone—just getting back?"

"Yes," said Father Martyn. "They have all returned safely, although your father is not entirely sound."

"What happened?" she asked as the priest removed a soiled stocking from T.J.'s left leg.

"During the raid, I caught some friendly fire," T.J. explained.

"Lindsey, have you any clean water?" Father Martyn asked.

When she leaned closer to see what was the matter with T.J., she felt suddenly faint and swayed a little. Father Martyn caught her by the arm.

"Are you all right?" he asked.

"Yes, I'm okay," she said quickly. "I've always been a little squeamish around blood." But she knew it wasn't just the blood that caused her to feel dizzy when she was this close to her handsome teacher.

He smiled. "I understand. Can you still fetch water?"

"Yes, of course." Lindsey had just used all the water they kept in the house, but it only took her a few minutes to refill the wooden bucket. As she did, all around her the colonists buzzed with excitement and news about the raid. Lindsey couldn't wait to find out what had happened.

The water was heavy. Under its weight she staggered back to the cottage as quickly as she could, managing not to spill more than a cup on the way.

Father Martyn began to clean the deep and bloody gash on T.J.'s left calf. Lindsey tried to watch, but kept turning her head. She hated gross stuff. Still, she was curious.

"Uh, Father," she awkwardly addressed T.J., "what's friendly fire?"

"When your own men injure you by accident," he explained patiently.

"How did it happen?" Lindsey wished he had a more comfortable place to sit. The bench was so hard.

"Someone got a bit nervous and mistook me for an Indian," he said vaguely.

"Were you shot?"

He nodded.

"Thomas, I do not believe the bullet shattered your bone," Father Martyn told him. "It seems you have not lost much blood either. Lindsey, dear, have you any good, strong tea?"

"Hmm…" She wasn't sure.

"Yes." T.J. pointed toward the leather satchel he had dropped by the fireplace. "You will find some sassafras in there."

Father Martyn straightened up, and something that looked like a coin fell from his pocket to the earthen floor. Lindsey reached down to get it for him. She examined the object's fancy scroll work and odd lettering, then handed it back.

The priest smiled underneath his dark beard. "Dear Lindsey, you act as though you have never seen a casting counter before."

"I, uh, I am just always amazed at how pretty they are," she muttered, wondering what a casting counter was. She looked to T.J. for guidance. His expression seemed to say, "I'll tell you about it later."

Lindsey boiled water over the open fire. "So how did it happen?" she asked.

"Well, everyone was tense with expectation as we landed," T.J. began. "We all followed Captain Stafford, who launched an attack much earlier than we had imagined."

"Why was that, Thomas?" Father Martyn asked.

"Several Indians were sitting around a fire when we arrived. The captain had us open fire, taking the natives by surprise."

"Did you shoot at them?" Lindsey couldn't believe T.J. had it in him to hurt anyone. She was sure her face gave away her feelings. She had never been good at masking them.

"No, I was way in the back of the charge, Lindsey. The Indians then fled into an area thick with water reeds. One of them got shot."

"Fatally?" Father Martyn asked.

T.J. nodded. "I am afraid so. It all ended just about as quickly as it had started when we heard a native call out Captain Stafford's name. You can imagine his surprise! Immediately our advance halted. Then we caught sight of an Indian woman carrying a child in a back sling, pleading for mercy."

The priest scrunched his thick eyebrows. "Were these not

followers of our enemy Wanchese?"

"Wasn't he one of the Indians who went to England?" Lindsey interrupted.

"Why, of course, he was," T.J. said quickly, shooting a warning glance in her direction. "Everyone knows that story."

Lindsey got the unspoken message. She must be careful not to say anything that might seem out of place.

"Do not fret, my child," Father Martyn said. "Many of our numbers believe Wanchese has turned on us like an unfaithful hound. However, I am not convinced."

Lindsey simply shrugged. The water was boiling now, and she wasn't sure what to do.

"Hand me the satchel, will you, Lindsey?" T.J. asked. He went through it and brought out some bark shavings which he handed to her.

Agnes Wood always made the tea for Mistresses Dare and Harvie. Lindsey didn't know what to do with the bark. Then she remembered how her mother sometimes bought loose tea. She put it in some kind of metal holder and dipped it into the hot water. There was nothing like that in this kitchen, though. She ended up plopping the bark into a clunky mug, then filling it with hot water and handing it to T.J.

"I see you have not learned the culinary arts," Father Martyn teased.

"I have not done well in that department," T.J. admitted.

"Perhaps Mistress Wood will help our Lindsey, then. She is a good domestic woman, and Lindsey will need those skills soon."

Lindsey wasn't sure what they were talking about, but she could guess, and she didn't like the sound of it.

"So, good friend, what happened next?" the priest asked T.J.

"To our dismay we quickly learned that these Indians were not followers of Wanchese. They were Croatoans."

"Manteo's people!" Father Martyn exclaimed.

"Indeed." T.J. nodded. "They had heard that the enemy Indians had fled, leaving their corn and fruit behind. The Croatoans, whose crops have not been plentiful, had gone to gather it up."

"How could Captain Stafford not know it was them?"

"When they asked for an identifying badge a week ago, the Croatoans were not given one."

"This is dreadful," Father Martyn muttered. "How did our friend Manteo take this?"

"He was upset, naturally. But he told Governor White that if the Croatoans' leader had kept his word to assemble the hostile Indians, this would not have happened."

Lindsey didn't like the dark expression on the priest's face.

"The Croatoans are our only friends. Manteo is one of our dearest numbers." Father Martyn shook his head sadly. "I pray God that this does not lead to disaster."

Chapter Seven

T.J. slept soundly the rest of that day, but Lindsey stayed at his side. She didn't like his bleached color, like old bones in a desert. When Father Martyn left, he promised to tell Agnes Wood and Bess that she wouldn't be there to help.

There was so much Lindsey wanted to ask T.J., and she needed his advice as to what to do about Andrew. She didn't trouble him, however. She knew sleep would help him heal.

Then, late in the slow, humid afternoon, Agnes Wood paid a surprise visit to the Wakesnoris cottage.

"Hello, Mistress Wood," Lindsey greeted her, wondering what had brought the woman to their cottage.

"I heard about yer father," the heavyset woman bellowed as she thumped her way through the door. She carried a rectangular basket as wide as she was. She made herself at home, plopping it on the table.

T.J. stirred restlessly, and Lindsey sniffed the air at yet another unpleasant smell; either Mistress Wood or her supplies reeked!

"I thought ye might be needin' some victuals," the woman said a little more quietly.

"Well, I…" Lindsey faltered.

"After all, I have not taught ye to cook yet, all except for some gruel." She reached into the basket that was half-filled with food.

"Yes, I was wondering—"

"I also heard about yer father's injury. He will be needin' one of my poultices for that." She lifted out a vile-looking cloth package—the source of the terrible smell.

Lindsey gaped at the poultice. "I don't think—"

"So, have ye a fire ready?" Agnes went on. "Yes, I see that ye do. Ye'll need to stoke it, girl! Ye cannot be leavin' a fire to tend to itself."

Lindsey rushed about the hearth as Agnes Wood barked orders non-stop. T.J. called to the old woman from the bunk, and Mistress Wood went over to him.

"How are ye feelin', Master Wakesnoris?" she asked loudly.

"I, uh, I..." He turned his nose up. "What is that terrible odor?" He tried sitting up, but Mistress Wood shoved him back on the bunk.

"Let me put this here poultice on yer wound," she said. "Where is it anyway?"

"Uh, I would rather not—"

"Now, I know it be a bit fragrant, but it will do ye good," the woman assured him.

T.J. pointed to his injured leg.

"Ah, yes." She nodded. "This will be just right for ye."

Lindsey hovered over the pushy woman as she arranged the stinky poultice on T.J.'s leg. When she finished, Mistress Wood ordered Lindsey back to the fireplace.

"Now then, Lindsey," she prodded, "I got this soup started. Ye'll have to finish it, though. A number of our people have come down with stomach complaints. I must be makin' the rounds of them. No one else can care for them like Mistress Wood."

"Wh-what should I do?" Lindsey asked.

She stared blankly into the cast-iron pot, which contained pieces of chicken with the skin and feathers still on. There was also an onion, some potatoey-looking vegetables, and water. Back home whenever a neighbor brought chicken soup, it came in a plastic container.

"Just stir it now and then. And for goodness' sake, Lindsey, keep the fire hot. I have taken care of everythin' else. I also brought yer father a bit of goat's milk." Mistress Wood looked immeasurably pleased with herself. "T'ain't much of it, ye know," she added slyly, "but I can git what I need. I also managed some biscuits. They are not what I would make at home, mind you. Still, they will be good enough for here and now." She sighed. "Ah, for my English hearth! Aye! For a hearth in Chesapeake where that rogue of a captain Fernandes should have taken us. Well then, I had best be goin' to the others. If ye be needin' anythin', ye come find me."

Lindsey watched her waddle through the narrow door sideways with the huge basket. What a woman!

"Lindsey," T.J. called as soon as Mistress Wood had gone.

"Yes, T.J.?" She hurried to his side.

"This poultice thing is horrible. Throw it out, will you?"

"Gladly." She lifted it from her teacher's leg with a grimace, then ran it out to a garbage dump near the house. When she returned seconds later, she frowned at T.J. "That thing must be as old as Mistress Wood."

"Old, eh? Just how old do you think she is?" T.J.'s eyes twinkled.

"She must be at least seventy!"

"Seventy," he repeated. "Lindsey, Mistress Wood is your parents' age."

"No!" Then, after it sank in she asked, "Why does she look so old?"

T.J.'s green eyes filled with compassion. "She's lived a hard life."

Lindsey couldn't imagine looking twice your age. These colonists sure didn't know much about good food, cleanliness, or staying young. "Do you need anything before I get to my cooking, T.J.?" she asked.

"Just some sleep."

But that wasn't to be. Just then Ben came through the door. "Was that Agnes Wood?" he asked, wrinkling his nose.

"Was she big and bossy?" Lindsey teased.

"Uh-huh. Man, you were right about her breath!" Ben fanned his face. "I've met sweeter skunks!"

"Yeah, well your breath isn't much better," Andrew said as he bounded into the room.

"Andrew!" Lindsey cried. "Where've you been!"

"Thanks for the greeting," he said sourly.

"No, it's just that I'm happy to see you." She didn't hug him, though. He didn't look like he wanted to be hugged.

"I talked him into coming home, such as it is," Ben explained. "George Howe promised him an adventure. Then he ran out on Andrew."

"He did not," Andrew argued. "He had something important to do."

"Hello, boys!" T.J. called out from the bunk.

"T.J.!" Ben rushed over to him. "You look really awful. What happened?"

The teacher grinned. As Lindsey struggled with the chicken soup, T.J. repeated his story for the boys.

Andrew wasn't sympathetic. "Well, Lindsey, I'm not going to sleep on that table just because our teacher is in your bed."

"That's awful!" Lindsey started arguing with her brother, but T.J. cut it short.

"Tonight I will sleep on the table as usual," he said. "But I will require your mattress, Andrew."

"You can use mine," Ben offered. "In fact, you can use our bunk if you like."

"Ben!" Andrew yelled.

"No, I'll stay on the table," T.J. said. "Andrew's mattress will do just fine. Now, go help your sister."

He glanced at Lindsey, who was busily pulling feathers from the chicken pieces. She was not in the least enjoying this dirty deed.

As they sat down to supper that night, Lindsey asked T.J., "What was that coin Father Martyn dropped?"

"It's called a casting counter. The colonists use them like we would a calculator." T.J. pulled a small feather from his mouth. The chicken soup was so watery and the vegetables so stringy that none of them ate more than a few spoonfuls.

"Are they used as money, too?"

T.J. shook his head. "Their sole purpose was calculation."

"I've seen men using them," Ben said. "I wondered what they were, too."

"So how did they work?" Lindsey asked.

"To make calculating easier the colonists set up counting surfaces with lines and spaces," T.J. said. "Each of them meant a different value. They'd keep a container of casting counters nearby to solve basic math problems on the counting surface."

"That's weird," Andrew said.

T.J. shrugged. "It's what they did. Now if you'll excuse me, I'm feeling tired."

Lindsey started cleaning off the kitchen table. When she finished, she and Ben put Ben's mattress on the table. T.J. stretched his tall body out on it, his long legs hanging over the edge. He looked uncomfortable, but he fell right to sleep anyway.

The next morning she found her teacher refreshed enough to attend chapel. Other colonists did not make the morning prayer service, however. Sickness had fallen upon them. Roughly one-fourth of the 116 colonists suffered from fevers and stomachaches. Because of this, the worshippers' numbers were down by a third.

Lindsey perspired freely under her heavy clothes. Was she sick, too? It was probably just the heat. Too bad Bess didn't pack shorts and T-shirts when she came here.

Lindsey listened closely as Governor White stood to make an announcement.

"I would like to thank all of you for your prayers during our recent expedition," the handsome man said in a strong, clear voice. "We have all returned. I am especially pleased that we suffered only one injury and that, not grievous." He nodded toward T.J. Lindsey blushed as she felt the dozens of eyes on her "family."

"We are extremely grateful to God for our safety and for the guidance of our dear friend, Manteo." White opened his hand to the Indian, who rose and stood next to the governor.

Lindsey studied the young man's interesting outfit, a combination of Indian and English designs. Although he wore breeches and a leather vest, Manteo's brown chest showed through. Odd tattoos ran down his arms, reminding Lindsey of interstates on a map. His calves were also bare, but Manteo wore a pair of leather shoes with silver buckles. A series of oyster shell beads circled his long neck. He wore his straight black hair in a ponytail.

Lindsey found herself wondering how old he was. He stood so regally that he could have been quite mature. His features were so smooth and unspoiled, though, that Manteo was probably more like twenty.

"Manteo has become a dear friend since our first meeting and his trip to fair England," the governor continued. "These last few days, his advice was priceless. For this I proclaim Manteo Lord of Roanoke under Sir Walter Raleigh, in the name of our sovereign, Queen Elizabeth, and before Almighty God, the maker of every race on earth."

Lindsey chuckled to herself at the way Governor White had pronounced Sir Walter Raleigh's name "Rall-eye."

Manteo bowed respectfully to the colony's leader. Then they shook hands.

Wow! thought Lindsey. She remembered reading about this, but seeing it firsthand was so cool. She sat forward on the hard bench, almost forgetting about the sweltering heat and her bug bites.

The governor turned to the priest now. "Manteo has requested Christian baptism," he said.

Father Martyn smiled broadly as the Indian moved to the wooden baptismal font. The priest said some lengthy prayers in old English and then gave instructions to the people. Lindsey found it difficult to understand what was going on. Father Martyn finally got to the baptism.

"Well-beloved, you have come hither desiring to receive holy Baptism," he read from the Book of Common Prayer. "We have prayed that our Lord Jesus Christ would vouchsafe to receive you, to release you from sin, to sanctify you with the Holy Ghost, to give you the kingdom of heaven, and everlasting life." He looked steadily at Manteo. "Dost thou renounce the devil and all his works, the vain pomp and glory of the world, with all covetous desires of the same, and the sinful desires of the flesh, so that thou wilt not follow, nor be led by them?"

Manteo spoke firmly and steadily. "I renounce them all, and by God's help, will endeavor not to follow, nor be led by them."

"Dost thou believe in Jesus the Christ, the Son of the Living God?"

"I do," Manteo said stalwartly.

After a few more questions, Father Martyn declared, "Manteo, I baptize you in the name of the Father, the Son, and the Holy Ghost. Amen." As he spoke these words, the priest scooped water from the font, splashing it over Manteo's head. The Indian didn't flinch as the liquid rolled down his forehead.

"He'll be the death of us yet," Lindsey heard Andrew whisper to Ben.

She felt like slapping her brother.

Ben was also irritated. "What are you babbling about?"

"Who do you think is making the colonists sick?" Andrew asked darkly.

Chapter Eight

Lindsey watched during the next week as T.J.'s condition improved. It heartened her to see him moving around more comfortably, going to chapel, and performing small household chores. Unfortunately Andrew's attitude worsened. On and on he groused about the heat, his uncomfortable clothes, the smells, and the food. Then he'd rail against T.J.— behind his back—threatening to get him fired if and when they got home.

T.J. hadn't said much to reassure them. "I pray so," was his answer whenever Andrew or Ben asked if they would soon be heading home. Lindsey was so caught up in the drama of the Lost Colony that she wasn't in a real hurry to return to her own time.

One day she heard Andrew mutter, "Pray all you want, but I don't see God anywhere. We only have ourselves to depend on."

"Andrew's up to something," Ben told her later.

"I know, but what?"

"He's still hanging out with that George Howe. They talk constantly about getting out of here." Ben pushed his phantom glasses up on his nose. He knew they weren't there, but he forgot and did it anyway.

"Well, they can't," she retorted. "Andrew can't return to our century, and George can't go back to England."

"That's not it," Ben said, sounding almost panicky. "I think they want to leave with Captain Fernandes when he pulls out in a few days. You know what that means! And we have to stick together."

"I agree." Lindsey nodded soberly. "We might never get back if Andrew gums up the works."

"We can't let Andrew run away." He pronounced each word slowly as he stared at Lindsey. "We have to get home!"

Lindsey grew suddenly quiet. She wished she knew what God was doing. It was one thing to be part of history—another thing entirely to be stuck in a time not your own.

Throughout that week the weather was either steamy or stormy with blaring thunder and vivid lightning. Lindsey stayed inside most of the time, caring for Mistresses Dare and Harvie. Bess's mother, Rose Payne, was to be their midwife, though Lindsey wondered how qualified she was. She knew they didn't have hospitals back then, but she was concerned that Mrs. Payne hadn't had much experience.

"I may have need of you, Bess and Lindsey," the tiny woman with the high-pitched voice told them one day.

Energetic and fussy, she seemed to Lindsey an only slightly older version of Bess. Unlike many of the other adult women at Roanoke, Rose Payne had not aged quickly.

"What about Mistress Wood?" Lindsey asked. She was excited about the impending births, but she didn't know the first thing about nursing. Nor did she like anything messy.

"Agnes will help me with the labor if the good physician is not at hand. We will need help with chores, though, and,"

Mistress Payne smiled roguishly, "with Master Dare. He is a wreck of a man these days." She sighed loudly. "Are not we all? Where will our troubles end? We have few supplies, and we are friendless in this God-forsaken place."

Mistress Payne seemed immediately sorry for her words when she saw Bess's forlorn expression. "Not to worry," she soothed, stroking her daughter's cheek. "God may have forsaken this place, but he will never leave or forsake us."

But Bess seemed only mildly comforted. Thankfully the girl didn't have much time to brood. The pregnant women demanded most of her attention. Neither expectant mother seemed in a hurry to deliver. Lindsey ministered to them as the young women suffered in the intense humidity. She gave them cool drinks and wiped their sweat-streaked faces. Mistresses Dare and Harvie were so great with child that they didn't get around much either. Dr. Humphrey Newton, the colonists' grey-haired physician, had advised them not to try.

"It is better for you to stay in your rooms," Lindsey heard him tell the women.

He had other reasons, too. "I am concerned about the spread of fever and stomach ailments through the settlement," he told Margery Harvie one day. He failed to see Lindsey standing in the shadows nearby. "You and Mistress Dare must not subject yourselves to it."

Lindsey and Bess didn't catch the illness. Dozens of other colonists were not as fortunate.

"It's that rotten savage's fault," Andrew said as he, Lindsey, and Thomas Archard left morning prayers one day. T.J. had remained behind with Ben. The teacher wasn't up to heavy labor yet, so he and Ben fished for the colonists' food. Manteo had shown them how to make a special kind of trap.

"Manteo is neither rotten, nor a savage," Lindsey said angrily.

"What makes you think Manteo has made our people sick?" Thomas asked Andrew.

"You don't know?"

Thomas shook his head. "I do not."

"He's poisoning the wells. People drink that water!"

Lindsey rolled her eyes. "That's ridiculous." She was embarrassed at Andrew's behavior.

"Have you evidence?" Thomas asked.

Andrew hesitated. Then he nodded smugly. "Yes, I do."

"Then you have seen Manteo do this abominable thing?"

"I haven't, but George Howe has."

Thomas was clearly unimpressed. "George Howe is not trustworthy. Do not you recall how much mischief he made on the voyage here?"

Of course he didn't remember! Before Andrew could put his foot in his mouth, Lindsey said, "He certainly did get into trouble."

"He has become even worse since the unfortunate death of his father," Thomas told them.

But Andrew wouldn't give up. "Who's to say that wasn't Manteo's doing, too?"

"Put a sock in it, Andrew!" Lindsey snapped. She reddened when Thomas looked at her curiously.

"I pray you to consider what you are saying." Thomas seemed to be growing impatient with Andrew.

"If everyone did less praying and more doing around here, we'd all be better off," Andrew said, then ran off.

"I would watch him closely if I were you," Thomas told Lindsey.

"Believe me, I am," she said. "Ben and I told him—"

Suddenly an ear-piercing cry split the air.

"W-what was that?" Thomas stammered.

"I think it came from the Dares' cottage. I'll bet she's having her baby." Lindsey gathered up her skirts and dashed off in the direction of the young couple's home, where she found Bess standing at the door. Ananias Dare paced in the background.

"There you are!" Bess cried just as another loud moan escaped from the cottage.

"Is Mistress Dare having her baby?"

"Yes, and she is having a difficult time. Mother is with her now and may need our help."

"What about Dr. Newton?"

"He is sick now, too."

"Oh, that's just great!" Lindsey groaned.

"Do you think Mistress Dare will be all right?" Bess asked, wringing her apron.

"I sure hope so."

Lindsey opened the door, but Bess couldn't seem to move.

"Are you okay, Bess?" she asked gently.

"I...I...I am afraid," she stuttered. "Mother wants me inside with her, but I am not looking forward to that."

"I guess not. I am sure you will be a big help to her, though." Lindsey smiled and squeezed the girl's slender arm.

"May I call upon you if Mother needs you, too?"

"Sure," Lindsey said more eagerly than she felt.

Bess started to go inside the cottage, but then she spotted Ananias Dare, who stalked about like a spooked horse.

"Methinks he may need someone to talk to. Do try to calm him, Lindsey."

"I will do my best," she said cheerfully. "I will make sure he does not go barging into the cottage."

Bess smiled wistfully. "I do hope the child will be a girl. Mistress Dare has her heart set on it."

Lindsey started to say, "Don't worry, she will," but stopped just in time. "I hope so, too." She grinned.

Lindsey approached Ananias Dare and began chattering about anything that came to her mind. She spent the entire day with him, pacing back and forth near the cottage. Around noon a soft rain began to fall, and they sat under a tree to avoid getting wet. Lindsey was grateful that he didn't try to go inside the cottage, since then she'd have to go in with him. She only went near the door when Bess leaned out to give periodic updates. Underneath the suspense, however, she was very excited. Lindsey was about to be present at the birth of Virginia Dare!

She and Master Dare had pleasant company during the day from well-wishers. Several people paid him visits, including Father Martyn and Dyonis Harvie. Mistress Dare's father, Governor White, stopped by frequently as he went about his busy schedule. Even Manteo came bearing a gift.

"You may give these herbs to Mistress Dare should the pain worsen," the Indian told Ananias.

"What is it?" Ananias's eyes narrowed as he sniffed the greens.

"An herb that my people have used for many years," Manteo explained. "It helps our women in childbirth."

"Is it poisonous?"

Manteo looked offended. "I would not give it to you if it was."

"Of course you wouldn't, Manteo," Lindsey said quickly. She was surprised at Ananias Dare's behavior.

"Thank you," the father-to-be said stiffly. Although Ananias accepted the weedy-looking objects from Manteo, Lindsey could tell that he had no intention of using them.

When Agnes Wood saw the remedy a little later, she threw it to the ground with contempt. "I'll not have that savage killing my patients."

Now Lindsey was really angry. She just couldn't see how her brother and that stupid George Howe or anyone else for that matter could think Manteo was dangerous. He was so gentle and caring. She wondered how Manteo put up with these suspicious, ungrateful people!

At seven-thirty that evening Virginia Dare announced her birth with a rousing cry. Ananias's ears perked up, and without a word to Lindsey, he burst through the door of his home. Lindsey didn't try to prevent him. Instead she waited quietly for news with T.J., Father Martyn, Ben, and Thomas Archard, who had come to keep her company. Some other healthy colonists also had braved the rain, which poured harder, to wait and pray.

Agnes Wood came out a few minutes later, declaring in a loud, happy voice, "It is a fine baby girl!"

A joyous shout rose from the people.

A half hour later Lindsey saw the first English child born in America. The healthy baby had thick blond hair and a cry to match her grandfather's booming voice. The news brought hope to the colony, to people who needed every opportunity they could get to rejoice.

Chapter Nine

The crowd milling around the Dare cottage finally began to thin, and Thomas Archard's mother stepped forward, inviting Lindsey and her family to dinner.

"Won't you share our supper with us?" asked the plump woman with hair as curly and blond as her son's. Mistress Archard's round brown eyes were friendly, though drawn.

"Mother has been wanting to invite you for oh, so long," Thomas added eagerly.

"I do apologize for our lack of hospitality," Arnold Archard said. Thomas's father was tall and stout. "In England we would have been quicker to ask. Here," he lowered his voice, "things are not the same."

Lindsey watched how Thomas refused to allow that note of sadness to ring for long. He was obviously excited about having her and her family for a visit.

"We do not wish to put you to any trouble," T.J. said. "We know how scarce food has become."

Lindsey was proud of how he'd learned to speak like the colonists. She wished it came that easily to her. She was forever using contractions and slang words.

"'Tis no trouble." Joyce Archard waved her chubby right hand. "Goodness, it is our duty to invite our son's intended and her family to our home."

Lindsey's jaw dropped. Her son's intended!

All eyes were on her. T.J. was watching her with amusement, and Ben's eyes were bugged out as he waited for her reaction. Arnold Archard grinned at her. This was too much. Is that how they did things here? You think someone's cute, and the next thing you know, you're married to him?

"Let us be off, then, before the rains melt us," Mistress Archard said, interrupting Lindsey's confusing thoughts. "Dear Lindsey has labored nearly as hard as Mistress Dare herself today. We cannot be expecting the young lass to prepare a meal, too."

"No, we cannot." T.J. smiled as they rushed along. "And I am very pleased with her work today."

Lindsey blushed, but she was grateful for T.J.'s compliment. "Thanks, uh, Father," she said, grinning.

"Will your other son be joining us this day?" Master Archard's keen eyes probed the area for a glimpse of Andrew.

"I am afraid he is otherwise engaged," T.J. answered stiffly.

Lindsey felt embarrassed. She wished her teacher would exercise more authority over Andrew. Still, T.J. was weak from the bullet wound. He didn't have the energy to go running after an eleven-year-old.

She, Ben, and T.J. followed the Archards to their newly-built cottage. Lindsey found the house in general disarray. Thomas's parents moved about quickly, removing items from benches so their guests could sit.

"The house was just completed two days ago," Mistress Archard explained breathlessly as she tidied up. "Is it not fortunate that Governor Lane's men built some homes when they were here?"

Lindsey, T.J., and his other two "children" nodded.

"You must excuse our disorder." Lindsey smiled as the older woman stuffed a linen cloth and spools of brown wool yarn into a corner. "Just last evening Arnold and Thomas brought our goods from the ship. I have been organizing all the day. Still, I am much behind."

"Please don't give it a second thought," T.J. said kindly, then grimaced slightly as he shifted his weight on the hard seat. Lindsey wished she had her dad's heated leather recliner at hand.

"I was so busy today, betwixt and between my home and tending to the sick. Is not it terrible how many have fallen ill?" Mistress Archard lowered her voice. "I hear there may be a problem with the water supply."

Lindsey glanced at Ben. Was Andrew spreading more rumors about Manteo? At least Thomas Archard didn't believe them. Maybe he could talk sense to his mother.

"Thomas, please see to the fire so that we may all dry off," Mistress Archard said.

Thomas smiled tenderly at Lindsey as he went about his task, and she found herself smiling back. He was cute. Still, she certainly didn't want to marry him! She suddenly wondered how he would look in jeans and a T-shirt. She almost giggled as she pictured Thomas rollerblading down her street in Williamsburg in his present outfit.

Lindsey sniffed as the cottage began to smell strongly of wood smoke. She thought about the economic status of the Archards. Their belongings were simple and few. Lindsey guessed that back in England they were hard workers who left in search of better opportunities or religious freedom. When a sudden gust of wind shook the windowless house, she looked up to see if the thatched roof had held. It had.

"My, how she blows!" Master Archard exclaimed. Then he asked, "How are you feeling, Thomas?"

An uncomfortable silence fell over the room before Lindsey realized that Archard was addressing T.J. and not his son. Obviously T.J. still wasn't used to being called "Thomas." She nudged him.

"What? Oh, I am terribly sorry, Arnold. What did you say?"

"I asked how you are feeling." He pointed to T.J.'s leg. "Your wound."

"I am doing better, thank you."

Dinner was served an hour later, and there wasn't much of it. Lindsey wasn't even sure what it was. Nevertheless she enjoyed the dish very much. Maybe she didn't even want to know what it was. She stared at her empty plate when she had finished. For the first time since arriving at the Lost Colony, she had enjoyed a meal.

"Back in England I always prepared game pie for company," Mistress Archard told her wistfully. "With it I served fresh greens and a nice trifle for dessert. I shall need to find new receipts here."

Lindsey didn't know what trifle or receipts were. This made her uncomfortable since ordinarily she knew so many things.

After the meal the Archards served sassafras tea, which looked and tasted a lot better than the kind Lindsey had made for T.J. after he was wounded. What had she done wrong? she wondered.

Master Archard was in a talkative mood. He eagerly shared

all he had learned that day from one of Governor White's assistants. The colony's leader and Captain Fernandes had been discussing some important matters, and Arnold Archard had heard some of what the men had said.

"The captain claims that a terrible storm is about to blow. From the sounds of the wind howling tonight, I would guess it has come upon us. Already the boats have been tossed about in these shallow waters. Aye, this place will be a graveyard for ships yet."

"I heard talk like that today, too," Ben said. He was back to working on the ships while T.J. and Father Martyn fished for the colony's food.

"Does that mean Ben and I will have a respite from working with the ship's crew?" Thomas asked.

"Nay. You and Ben, and probably Andrew, will haul wood and fresh water to the ships for their homeward journey. There will be caulking and trimming of the vessels as well."

Lindsey saw the blank look on Ben's face. He had no idea what that meant. She hoped it wasn't as hard or nasty as it sounded.

"Dear Lindsey, will you be tending to Mistress Harvie tomorrow?" Joyce Archard asked.

"I guess so," she replied. No one had told her otherwise.

"We may have need of her elsewhere," Mr. Archard announced. "Governor White mentioned just today that it is time we write letters if we wish to send any back to England. The ships mean to sail three days from today. Captain Fernandes will see to it that our messages are delivered." He seemed to enjoy knowing what was going to happen.

But his wife didn't seem impressed. "Humph," she retorted

while refilling their cups. "He has not proven to be a man of his word yet. He brought us here, did he not, when we were to go north to the Chesapeake?"

"Aye, but how else will we send messages if not through the captain?"

"I heard today that one of us colonists is to return to England with Captain Fernandes," Thomas said earnestly. "That way our letters will make it to their intended recipients."

"Aye, but 'tis not for letters alone," his father corrected. "We be fearfully low on provisions."

"Yes, especially we are low on victuals," Ben said trying to sound like a real colonist.

Lindsey bit her cheek to keep from laughing.

"You do speak strangely sometimes, Benjamin." Thomas smiled.

"I...uh...I..."

Lindsey stepped in. "Who will be sent to England?"

"Possibly one of the governor's assistants," Master Archard replied. "That makes the most sense." He became quiet, stroking his dark blond beard peppered with dull gray. "Some say the governor himself."

"Why, Father?" Thomas asked, his eyebrows raised.

"He carries the most authority and is a persuasive leader of men. If he were to return, Sir Walter Raleigh would be apt to listen."

"Aye, and he would urge that rogue of a Captain Fernandes on to England," added Mistress Archard. "Otherwise he may live out his days privateering."

"There is just one problem," Thomas said. "Who, then, will be our colony's leader? We have need of a strong man. You know how we have bickered amongst ourselves."

"Ah, there is the rub." His father sighed.

A while later as they walked home in the dark, Ben teased Lindsey mercilessly. "Dear Lindsey this and Dear Lindsey that," he mimicked Mistress Archard. "We had a duty to invite our son's intended and her family."

"Oh, cut it out!" She punched his arm.

"I think Thomas is going to marry you if we don't get out of here."

"Is that true, T.J.?" Lindsey demanded.

He nodded. "That's the impression I got."

"But I'm only thirteen! Besides, this is a free country, and I'll marry when and who I please." She was furious to think her rights didn't matter.

"You're forgetting, Lindsey, that America isn't even here yet." Ben grinned.

Lindsey became concerned. "So, this is real, huh?"

"I told you earlier that in this society you're an adult," T.J. said. "Marriage is right around the corner for a girl your age."

His tone was teasing, but Lindsey wasn't laughing.

Agnes Wood cornered Lindsey and Bess after chapel the following day. The rain had stopped, but the wind still snapped. "You are needed today to collect mail from our numbers," she said.

"But I wish to assist Mistress Dare," Bess protested.

The woman refused to budge. "I have everything under control. You young ones are susceptible to illness. We must keep you from the infant for a spell."

"Who will tend to Mistress Harvie?" Bess asked hopefully.

"Ah, girl, you do have a point," the bossy woman agreed. "Let you go to the Harvies."

"Cannot another go in Lindsey's stead," Bess pleaded, "that we may stay together?"

"My, ye are persistent!" Mistress Wood exclaimed. "Would ye have me do it meself?"

"No, no," Lindsey insisted. "I would prefer to collect the mail, uh letters."

"Be gone, then," Mistress Wood said. "And keep yerself covered against these buffeting winds. When ye have finished this task, Mistress Harvie will likely be delivered of her babe. Then ye may help Bess again."

Although Bess moped over the loss of Lindsey's company, Lindsey didn't mind. She didn't want to be cooped up in the Harvie's cottage getting bossed around by Agnes Wood all day. And so, for the next three days she gathered mail for the departing ship to take back to England. Nearly every family and individual had letters to send. Father Martyn had announced in chapel that now was the time to write them. Those who had missed services because of illness learned of this through the priest's and Lindsey's visits. Many colonists couldn't read or write, so she gladly composed their letters for them. She loved hearing all the interesting things people had to say about life on Roanoke Island.

Not so happily Lindsey also learned on her travels that about twenty people had died of the stomach illness and fever. The news had been kept quiet to avoid a panic. T.J. told Lindsey that the cause of death was probably dysentery. Severe shipboard conditions and malnourishment were the likely causes, not poisoned water. Still, the rumors about Manteo persisted, and so the Indian stayed very much in the background. Lindsey felt sorry for him, and whenever she could, she told people how highly she regarded him. And she carried her own secret concerns. T.J.'s wound wasn't healing properly, and her brother was still sulky and mean-spirited.

Then, on a dark, rainy afternoon in August, Lindsey returned from her duties to find Ben dripping all over the dirt floor, speaking rapidly, and making lots of hand motions to T.J., who listened with a concerned expression on his face.

"What's wrong?" she asked.

When Ben spotted her, he rewound his message like a tape player. "Didn't you hear, Lindsey?"

"Hear what?" Something about the way he looked gave her the creeps.

"Captain Fernandes left with the ships, and I can't find Andrew anywhere!"

Chapter Ten

For the next six days the Cittie of Raleigh was as stormy as the wind and rain lashing the colony. Many feared that once again Captain Fernandes had betrayed them. Governor White tried to reassure his people. He explained that Fernandes had to ride out the storm away from their shallow settlement.

"His boats would be battered to smithereens, and what good would that do anyone?" White asked.

Few were convinced.

"He was born a rogue, is a rogue, and always will be, world without end. Amen!" Agnes Wood proclaimed to Lindsey one afternoon.

"She is a fiercesome woman," John Wyles said as he visited the Wakesnoris cottage on one of those tempest-tossed nights. "She claims that Fernandes has left us for good. She and Richard Wildye have spread much discontent amongst us about this."

Lindsey knew beyond any doubt that the sea captain would return to Roanoke. History had proved that centuries ago. Nevertheless, she had cause for concern—Andrew had not returned since the day the captain's boats departed.

Manteo knew the island and its surroundings like the map of veins on his hands, and he had not seen Andrew either. Since George Howe also was missing, Lindsey believed that

Andrew had followed Howe in stowing away on the ship.

"Bad move," she remarked when they first discovered Andrew was missing. "He's trying to get home in the dumbest way! If he would've done his history homework, he would know that Captain Fernandes is going to return."

T.J. hung his head. "I've done it again," he murmured.

"Done what?" Lindsey asked.

"The parents at the high school couldn't trust me with their children either."

"Don't say that! You can't help it if you fall asleep. You certainly can't help that you got shot!"

"But none of it is an excuse for losing control of your brother." He shook his head sadly.

"That's like saying you could stop this rain by putting up an umbrella," Lindsey retorted. "My brother was an accident waiting to happen. No one can control someone like that."

But T.J. did not seem comforted.

Governor White had difficulty controlling the wagging tongues of Agnes Wood and Richard Wildye. Throughout that week they planted doubts about his leadership. One of their favorite rumors was to insist that White was untrustworthy because he believed in Manteo's innocence.

"Everyone knows Manteo has made dozens sick by poisoning our wells with his loathsome herbs," Richard Wildye declared to everyone. It didn't seem to matter to him that Dr. Humphrey Newton had said Manteo's herbal medicines were harmless.

"Actually, I have found some of them rather useful," the

doctor had told Governor White. "They have made my stomach ailment much improved."

Still, the frenzy prevailed.

Lindsey felt challenged by the chaos all around her, but she was also excited about being part of history. She did wish, however, that Thomas Archard wouldn't walk her to chapel every morning. People were beginning to talk, and Lindsey felt super uncomfortable about the whole thing.

In the midst of the uproar Lindsey kept busy urging people to write letters. She assured them that Captain Fernandes would return to the settlement after the weather calmed down. When they asked how she knew she always said, "Believe me. I just do."

In addition to her postal duties, she visited the sick with Father Martyn. Most of them believed Manteo had made them ill. Lindsey constantly fought the urge to tell them how stupid they were. Instead she said things like, "I am sure that Manteo, who is a Christian, would not do such a thing."

Ben stuck up for him as well. Since he didn't have any ships to unload, he and Thomas Archard spent a lot of time fishing with Manteo. They endured constant jibes from others over this. "Stick with him," Lindsey had advised. "He is an honest man and needs our support."

A couple of bright spots shone into their darkness. One Sunday in late August Father Martyn baptized Virginia Dare. This lifted almost everyone's spirits, especially when the priest referred to the child as a symbol of new beginnings.

Then Margery Harvie gave birth to a tiny boy weighing only five pounds. They named him Walter after Sir Walter Raleigh, the colony's sponsor. Because she was busy gathering letters, Lindsey had not been present at the little boy's birth.

The joy of these events was short-lived, however. Most of the colonists continued to complain bitterly about their primitive conditions. Many pined for the homes they had left in England.

When Governor White gave his word that Captain Fernandes would return, he asked that two of his assistants then accompany the seaman back to England. This created another firestorm. None of the assistants would comply.

John Wyles told Lindsey, T.J., and Ben privately at their cottage one day, "I would go if I knew it would help. Alas, it would not. Who am I that Sir Walter Raleigh would believe me?" He sighed. "I fear that only Governor White could convince him and Her Majesty to send supplies to us quickly."

"But wouldn't they accuse him of desertion?" Lindsey voiced White's own concern. "Wouldn't they say he abandoned his post?"

Wyles shrugged. "'Tis a possibility, but we must prevail upon him anyway. I know Sir Walter. He would not listen to the likes of me or any other assistant. He is not given to heeding the pleas of an inferior. Already he grows weary of this colony. His interest has waned this last year. Only Governor White is in a position to plead for us with good result."

"Have you expressed this to the governor?" T.J. asked.

"Oh, indeed, yes. We assistants have met with him several times. We have not convinced him, though."

"What happens next?" Lindsey asked.

"I believe we shall have a people's assembly to settle the matter." Master Wyles stood and reached for his hat and cloak. His cloak was made for cold weather, but Wyles used it to protect himself from the wind and the rain, which had turned the colony into a mud pit. "Do not you worry, my good friends." He smiled. "You have much on your minds with the absence of young Andrew. Let me worry on your behalf."

That was really nice of him, Lindsey thought, as she watched him slip out of the cottage. But how could she keep from worrying? What if the captain threw Andrew overboard or something, and because of that, they never got home? That night she prayed herself to sleep.

The next day a special assembly met in the chapel to settle the issue of who should return to England, representing the colonists. The persistent storm flung itself at the fragile building, while inside, residents of the colony verbally flung themselves at each other. Sitting with his parents several benches ahead and to the right, Thomas Archard caught Lindsey's eye and smiled. She returned the greeting, though not enthusiastically. At least he hadn't sat down beside her.

Governor White explained why he thought it would be unwise for him to return to England. "I will be discredited," he concluded after some minutes. "I will be criticized for leaving the action here. No one will then support us."

"Governor White has presented his case," Father Martyn said after the leader took his seat. "Now let us hear from those who wish to speak for or against his position."

The menacing Richard Wildye immediately jumped to his feet. He stuck out his chest, and for a moment Lindsey thought he was going to pound it like Tarzan.

"Already twenty-four of our numbers have died of mysterious ailments. Would you leave us to the savages, Governor, to a cruel fate worse than death? Indeed, you say yes if you refuse to return."

"Would not it be better if Governor White stayed to guide us?" Bess asked Lindsey quietly.

"We need his leadership more in England than here," Lindsey explained. "As Governor White said, his assistants wouldn't be taken seriously by the people who can help us."

Bess sighed. "'Tis too hard for a girl to understand."

"I don't see why," Lindsey retorted. "You are as smart as any boy."

Bess stared at her strangely as Ananias Dare rose to speak.

"Governor White—Father—I address you in a more benevolent spirit than my counterpart." He shot a spirited glance at Wildye. "But I believe you alone can help us." Everyone listened. "I think you must leave."

For a moment, Lindsey thought Governor White would back down. Then he said in a choked voice, "How can I leave my family, my responsibilities, my possessions? You should be moving northward to the Chesapeake soon, as we have discussed. How will I find you upon my return? And how will I find my possessions, my paints and brushes, all that I need to complete my precious drawings of America? As you travel, how will you protect the pictures I have made? Already someone here among us has seen fit to ransack my belongings whilst I was away from the settlement for a short time." His eyes pleaded with the colonists to understand his position.

"'Twas a tragedy," Dare agreed as the two men stood face-to-face. "But I give you my word as a gentleman, sir, that if we move north before your return, I will personally bury your treasures in a sturdy trunk under my very cottage. Moreover, I will guard with my life your greatest treasures—your daughter and our child."

The governor met Dare's eyes as he considered this offer.

"I would speak!" Richard Wildye broke the calm.

"You would listen!" Ananias turned on him heatedly. "I have not finished with my good father yet."

Wildye angrily plopped down on the bench with a thud. Served him right, Lindsey thought with a grin.

"My good son," Governor White turned to Ananias. "My possessions matter not a whit compared to the treasures of my daughter, yourself, and Baby Virginia. How will I find you if you move north before my return?"

"We will impose on the tree next to the chapel a message telling you of our destination," Ananias explained. "Furthermore, if we must leave in a hurry, we will carve a Maltese cross."

"And how will you perform this move?"

"Everyone but the single men among us should move to Chesapeake as soon as possible. Those men will stay behind to direct you upon your return. They will use this as a base of operations in the meantime."

Governor White considered this thoughtfully.

After a brief pause Ananias Dare asked, "Will you return to England, then, Father?"

To Lindsey, it was a foregone conclusion, but Governor White still hesitated. "Would you and the others draw up a document? In it will you swear that I have left only under the duress of your pleas because of our desperate situation? Will you do this so Her Majesty and Sir Walter do not find me guilty of desertion or politicking?"

Master Dare addressed the assembly. "Do you see fit to do so, friends?"

"Aye!" came the loud response, for a moment drowning out the rain that pounded against the roof.

"You have heard our intention, sir. Will you go?" Ananias asked hopefully.

"I will respond tomorrow."

"Goodbye, and God bless you!" Lindsey told the last colonist from whom she had collected mail. As she closed the door behind her, the sun poured its warmth over her like a bowl of grace. She stood for a moment to relish the feeling. It had been days since she had last seen the sun. Not even the mosquito that she smashed indelicately on her neck could quell her spirits today.

Suddenly Thomas Archard called to her from several yards away. "Lindsey! Captain Fernandes has returned with his ships!" As she drew closer to him, she thought he smelled like wet leather.

Although she had known Fernandes would return, Lindsey was excited to hear the news. She wondered if Thomas knew anything about Andrew. It was strange enough knowing the future before it came. What made it even weirder was how her family and T.J. fit into the drama.

"The captain says he must leave on the next tide."

"And Governor White will go with him?" she asked because it seemed the right thing to do.

"Yes. He agreed to it this morning. His assistants and Father Martyn drew up a document giving his reasons for leaving. They signed it in the governor's presence."

"When will he leave?"

"He only has a few hours to collect his belongings and say his farewells, poor man," Thomas explained. "Father asked if you are ready with the letters."

"I just collected the last one. What should I do with them?"

"Know you where Governor White lives?"

She felt like saying, "Of course. Doesn't everybody?" but she held her tongue and pointed to a cottage near the water.

"Then you may rush the letters to him at once, and I must assist the captain's crew. They brought in the small boats to convey wood and fresh water to the larger ones for the voyage."

They hurried along beside everyone else, who also seemed to be in a great rush.

"Thomas, have you seen my brother?" Lindsey asked. "Was he with the crew?"

"I think you are very soon to find out," he replied.

Chapter Eleven

rantic activity greeted Lindsey at the water's edge. Sailors who reminded her of the ones in *Treasure Island* shouted orders from the boats to the shore and vice versa. Men and boys scrambled to gather bundles of wood and casks of fresh water for the voyage.

"We haven't got all day," roared one sailor. "The captain wants out o' here before the shoals and storms tear these ships to pieces!"

"See there, Lindsey?" Thomas took her by the elbow.

"Where?" She felt like shaking him off but didn't want to be rude.

"Just beyond the shore to the left," he said.

Lindsey saw a small boat with several men and… "Holy cow!" she shouted. Her brother and George Howe were rowing one of the boats while sailors teased them mercilessly.

"Lindsey!" someone suddenly called.

She turned to find T.J. striding toward them.

"T.—" she started to say, then quickly corrected herself. "Father! Did you see Andrew?"

"Yes. Thank God he appears to be all right."

"If not in spirit." Thomas chuckled.

As the sailors anchored the craft, Lindsey, T.J., and Thomas rushed toward them. Two burly seamen picked up Andrew and George by their collars, then dropped them like sacks of corn on the sand.

"That should settle things!" One of the seamen laughed harshly. He slid his hands back and forth as if ridding them of dirt.

"Andrew!" Lindsey exclaimed.

He looked up, sputtering and spitting sand out of his mouth. He then tried rubbing it out of his eyes, but that just made it worse.

"Is this yours?" a toothless sailor asked T.J.

"Yes, he is mine."

"And this one?" He pointed to George.

"No."

Lindsey watched as Howe suddenly took off like a frightened rabbit. He ran into the woods outside the settlement.

T.J. tried to lift Andrew from the sand, but his face grew red from the effort. Thomas quickly stepped in to assist him.

"He tried stowin' away," the sailor said, "but we only takes seasoned men, not miscreants like this. He ain't got his sea legs, this one!" He roared at his own joke, then started shouting orders to his men.

Lindsey wondered what T.J. would do with her brother. She surprised herself by hoping he would take it easy on Andrew. He looked so defeated. Besides, now that they were all together again, they could eventually get back home. Lindsey was starting to miss the familiar comforts. Still, before she went home, she wanted to discover exactly what had happened with the lost colonists.

"Let us get you cleaned up, Andrew," T.J. said, his voice sternly gentle.

Lindsey tried to make eye contact with her brother, but he kept his eyes on the ground.

"Do you need help, Master Wakesnoris?" Thomas asked.

"No, thank you, Thomas," T.J. said. "You have your own work to do. Lindsey, were you busy doing something?"

She couldn't tell whether he wanted her help or not. "I was just going to deliver these letters to Governor White."

"Then carry on," he instructed. "If you will excuse us." He tipped his hat and slowly walked off with Andrew under tow. Her brother's legs wobbled, and T.J. helped him along with what strength he had.

"I am glad your brother is all right, Lindsey, if not exactly well," Thomas said.

"Me, too. I sure hope he never pulls something like that again."

"Was it for the adventure that he ran away?"

Lindsey became thoughtful. "I seriously doubt it." When she saw Thomas's questioning gaze she said, "Andrew likes getting his own way better than he likes adventures."

Thomas's dark blond eyebrows knit together as he seemed to try to make sense of this.

"I should deliver these letters," Lindsey hastily announced, and she started to walk away.

"Aye, and I had better help load the boats." He tipped his hat and smiled sweetly as their eyes met. "Good day."

She wished he wouldn't look at her like that. She hurried to the governor's cottage, where Eleanor Dare, red-eyed and carrying her crying infant, met her at the door.

"Lindsey," she said, sniffing away her tears, "how good to see you."

"Hello, Mistress Dare." Lindsey held out the stack of letters, reminding herself to speak formally. "I have gathered these from the colonists for Governor White to take to England."

"Do bring yourself in," the woman invited.

Lindsey stepped into a two-room cottage filled with Governor White's sketches of native American plants, animals, and people. She caught her breath at their beautiful simplicity. He had captured the spirit of the place perfectly. Lindsey remembered seeing some of his black and white sketches in her history book and liking them. Up close they leaped to life.

Governor White was in a tizzy, trying to decide what to take and what to leave behind. He grunted a greeting to Lindsey and continued working at a frantic pace.

Suddenly Eleanor's eyes brightened. "Lindsey, have you anything else to do just now?"

Lindsey was dying to get back to her cottage and find out what was going on with Andrew, but she decided it could wait.

"No. Is there something I can help you with?"

"Oh, yes, indeed! I so want to assist my father with his packing, but Virginia," she stressed each syllable so it came out Vir-gin-i-a, "needs my attention even more urgently. Will you tend to her while I assist him? She has just been fed. She simply needs to be cuddled and played with."

Lindsey held out her arms, and Mistress Dare placed the chubby infant in them. Then she flew about the cottage, giving her father a desperately needed hand. Lindsey bounced Virginia softly and spoke gently to her until the child stopped fussing. Suddenly the reality of the situation crashed into her mind like gale-force winds. "I'm actually holding Virginia Dare while her mother helps Governor John White pack for England!" This realization made her dizzy, and so she found part of a bench not covered with White's clothes, books, or drawings, and slowly sat down. No one back home would ever believe this.

An hour later the packing was finally finished, and Eleanor Dare, her baby, her husband, and her father walked together toward the shore. Lindsey then made a quick check of the cottage to make sure the governor had taken everything he wanted. Suddenly her eyes fell upon a small leather pouch he had dropped near the door. She picked it up, opened it, and saw that it contained a few dozen casting counters. She knew he would want them. She ran after his party, but as she neared the shore, she found she couldn't get past the crowd of seventy or so people who had gathered to see the governor.

Richard Wildye stood near Lindsey, and she could hear him telling Agnes Wood that Governor White would be traveling to England in the flyboat instead of with Captain Fernandes on the flagship *Lyon.*

"No doubt so the two of them do not cut each other's throats," Mistress Wood said.

"Well, at least we colonists get to keep the pinnace with its two boats," Wildye reflected.

Father Martyn's voice carried above the surf, seizing Lindsey's attention. "Dear brothers and sisters in Christ," he repeated until everyone grew quiet. "We have gathered to bid our honorable and beloved Governor White goodbye. Let us pray to Almighty God for his safe-keeping!"

Lindsey bowed her head as the priest prayed.

"Our Father in heaven, we thank thee for our dear Governor John White and for his willingness to return to fair England for our relief. We pray that you will give your angels charge over him and those who sail with him. Guard them in all their ways. Make their voyage smooth and sure. Meet all their needs according to your riches in glory in Christ Jesus."

People all around Lindsey cried softly as they murmured, "Lord, hear our prayers."

"Please grant him favor at the court of our beloved Queen Elizabeth," Father Martyn continued. "May our governor return to us soon with the supplies we need, not just to fill our bellies, but so that we may spread the love of your Son, Jesus Christ, throughout this new land. Father, it is in Jesus' precious name that we pray, amen."

"Amen," Lindsey muttered, sniffling. She watched as Governor White hugged and kissed his family. Then he shook the hands of his assistants and waved his hat at the colonists, wearing a gallant smile.

"I think that's what's called putting on a brave face," Ben said as he came to stand beside Lindsey. "What kills me," he whispered as they watched the governor depart, "is that he'll never see his family again."

Lindsey watched her cousin closely. Of course this would deeply affect him. One day two years earlier his father also had left on a trip and not returned.

"I think this is really bizarre, Ben," she said.

He cocked his head. "How so?"

"Well, here we are, four hundred years from home, watching history happen up close."

Ben sighed. "I know exactly what you mean."

"Now we get to see what became of these people," she said gleefully.

"Yeah. Since we had to go through this in the first place, we might as well find out how it ends." Ben obviously didn't share his cousin's enthusiasm. "Do you think our parents will fire T.J. when they find out what he's done?"

"I sure hope not!" she exclaimed. "Think of the adventures we'll miss if he leaves!"

Ben gaped at her. "I'd rather not," he said.

Chapter Twelve

"All anyone does is complain anymore." Bess Payne leaned wearily against a tree as she took a break from pounding corn into a fine flour. She covered the container so the wind wouldn't blow away any of the precious grain. Then she frowned. "Just listen to me, Lindsey! I, too, am full of complaints about complainers!"

"I understand," Lindsey sympathized. "Between the lack of supplies and arguments about what to do next, things have not been pleasant." Nor was doing this. Her hand ached from crushing corn with a pestle against the bottom and sides of a heavy stone mortar. If only she had her mother's food processor.

"No one is in charge, and everyone is in charge." Bess sighed and smoothed back a stray piece of brown hair. "I think Master Dare should be our leader because he is the son-in-law of the governor. Then again, I think highly of Master Wyles. Of course, anyone is better than that beast, Richard Wildye!" Bess kicked at the ground, startling a squirrel that scurried away. "You should hurry, little one," she told it, "or you will end up in Mistress Wood's pot!"

"I suppose Governor White should have named a leader before he left," Lindsey said carefully. She didn't want to add to the unhappiness that fouled the Cittie of Raleigh. "Still, he left in such a hurry."

"You know, Lindsey, he did name a leader!" Bess said excitedly.

"Oh?"

"Of course!" She lowered her voice and leaned close. Lindsey slowly drew away. Time had ripened Bess's body odor. "Governor White made Manteo Lord of Roanoke!"

"That's right!" Lindsey snapped her fingers. "But who would follow him, Bess? Half the people think he has poisoned the wells, which is ridiculous."

"So you believe in him, too?" Bess asked softly.

Lindsey stared at her friend in surprise. Bess believed in Manteo? She so often referred to him as a savage.

"Of course I do," Lindsey said. "He is a gentle and kind-hearted Christian. I doubt, though, that many would follow Manteo."

"I suppose you are right." Bess sighed. "In the meantime we wallow in our ignorance." Then she asked, "How soon do you think we will go to Chesapeake?"

"I don't know."

In the background Lindsey heard the sound of axes shaping a felled pine into a dugout. The slow process of burning and gouging had gone on for days now. This was done to properly hollow the canoe. Manteo supervised this operation, and although he was good at creating dugouts, not even he could make the operation go faster. In two weeks' time, they had only finished one canoe and were almost through with another.

Lindsey thought about her brother's work with Manteo on the dugouts. Each night since he had started the task, a gentler, quieter Andrew had returned to the cottage smudged with soot or bruised from the punishing work. He didn't complain, though. In fact, he hadn't said much at all since the sailors dumped him on the shore of Roanoke Island. He seemed to be changing a lot on the inside. Lindsey watched him in fascination. Could this nice kid really be her little brother?

"I suppose we would not all fit into the pinnace and its two boats," Bess went on. "A boat as small as a pinnace is not designed to carry an entire colony by itself."

"Besides," Lindsey added, "those who remain on Roanoke Island have to have transportation, too."

Bess grew thoughtful. "You are so smart for a girl. I could never aspire to your loftiness."

Lindsey coughed to keep from laughing.

"I just hope we leave before everyone dies. This place smells of death." Bess hugged herself and shivered.

Suddenly Lindsey didn't feel much like laughing. A great gray cloud bank creeping steadily toward them from the ocean highlighted Bess's spooky talk. The eerie effect gave her the shivers.

"I can do no more today," Bess announced. "I shall take my corn flour to Mistress Wood."

She began to gather her container and utensils, then stopped to stare for a long moment at Lindsey's dress, the dress she had loaned her. Lindsey shifted uncomfortably.

"Uh, Bess, if you would like your dress back…" she said slowly.

"I am all right," she said. "You have need of it."

"But you do, too, don't you? I mean, yours is smelling pretty awful these days." When Bess's face grew scarlet, Lindsey instantly regretted her bluntness.

"I…I had not noticed. I only wanted you to be comfortable," Bess said, and then she started to cry. She turned and began walking quickly away.

"Oh, Bess, I'm sorry!" Lindsey called after her. "I didn't mean it!" But by then Bess was too far away to hear Lindsey's apologies. "I sure blew that one," she scolded herself. "Why did I say such a stupid thing? I really hurt her feelings." She sighed. "I'll have to apologize again tomorrow."

When she finally finished grinding the corn into a coarse flour, she took it to Agnes Wood. The overbearing woman had begun rationing the colony's dwindling food supplies. Although she talked too much, everyone agreed she was a whiz at making a little food go a long way.

"Be careful out there, Lindsey Wakesnoris," she advised as Lindsey tried to leave for the fifth time. "And do not forget the stew for your supper."

"Okay, Mistress Wood," she chanted. She picked up the pot containing barely enough food for her and her family. A mosquito landed on her forearm, and she nearly spilled the stew trying to slap it.

"Do be careful with that!" Agnes Wood snapped. "We cannot be wastin' food!"

Lindsey rolled her eyes.

"Those heavy clouds out there mean trouble for sartain," the older woman said.

"Yes, Mistress Wood."

"Better lay low 'til tomorrow."

"Yes, Mistress Wood."

"Tell your father I will have a new poultice for his wound then," she added.

"Oh, he doesn't need it," Lindsey said quickly. "He is doing much better." She wrinkled her nose as she remembered the first one's revolting smell.

But Mistress Wood wasn't listening. "I will bring it to him first thing after chapel. Ah, I do not know why the good father bothers these days. So few come."

"Good-day," Lindsey called.

"Yes, and…"

Unable to take another whiff of Mistress Wood's breath or the torrential downpour of words, Lindsey fled. She hurried across the settlement to her cottage, dodging mosquitoes and another rain shower as she went. In spite of it all, she felt happier than she had in a long while. Andrew was back and behaving, and T.J. was on the mend. And if all continued to go well, they might soon find out what happened to the colonists.

After dinner that night, Ben helped Lindsey clear the pewter dishes from the table. Andrew washed them in a kettle over the fire. Their stomachs felt far from full, though, and Lindsey found herself craving a double-cheese pizza with extra pepperoni. She pictured it so vividly in her mind, right down to the steam rising from the hot, slightly browned cheese, that she could almost taste the oregano in the sauce.

"Some of the men have taken to eating just one meal a day," T.J. said as he dried the plates. "That way the women and children will have enough."

"I had no idea!" His news startled Lindsey out of her day-dream. "Agnes Wood tells me everything else. I wonder why she never mentioned that."

T.J. shrugged.

"She probably just hasn't worked her way down to that subject yet." Lindsey shook her head. "Can that woman ever jabber!"

T.J. smiled, which Lindsey thought was a good sign that

his health was improving. Then he said, "There's been a change of plans for tomorrow." But right then someone came to the door.

"Guess who?" Ben asked in a sing-song voice. He and Andrew exchanged impish grins.

"Well, it's not Domino's Pizza," Lindsey muttered.

"Thomas Archard's visits are becoming rather frequent." T.J. grinned, then went to the door and opened it. "Hello, Thomas. Come in out of the rain."

"Hello, everyone." Thomas removed his wet hat and hung it on a rack near the door. "I hope I am not intruding."

"No. In fact, I need to talk to you," T.J. said.

Thomas looked startled. "You do?"

"I was about to tell my, uh, children, that Captain Stafford will take several people to the mainland tomorrow. He thinks we can find fish and game there."

"Who's going?" Andrew asked.

"About twenty people, including John Wyles, us, and perhaps yourself," T.J. said. "I thought you could use a break from your chores."

"That would be great!" Lindsey smiled at the thought of a day away from Agnes Wood. Still, she did want to apologize to Bess for the crack about smelling bad.

"I'd like to go," Ben said.

Andrew remained quiet. Lindsey knew how much her brother enjoyed working on the dugouts. The physical labor was satisfying, and Manteo was a good teacher. Andrew spoke highly of the Indian now. He knew how wrong he had been about him.

"I would like to stay behind if I could," Andrew told T.J.

"Manteo and I are real close to finishing a canoe."

T.J. thought for a moment. "All right, Andrew," he said finally. "You may stay with Manteo." He turned to Thomas Archard then. "Your help would be appreciated."

"I will check with my father," he promised.

"Good! We leave at daybreak with the high tide, assuming the weather does not worsen."

"How long will we be gone?" Lindsey asked.

"Just for the day."

The following morning Lindsey found herself in a boat that rocked restlessly on the waves of Croatoan Sound. The wind had steadily increased overnight. With her were Ben, T.J., Thomas, John Wyles, and ten others. Everyone but Captain Stafford had expressed concern that a major storm was coming.

"We are going to the mainland!" he'd insisted. "We need food."

A concerned Manteo had approached the captain just before Stafford launched his own boat with nine men. Lindsey smiled at Andrew, who stood off to the Indian's side.

"Captain Stafford, I do not think you should go today," Manteo advised.

"It is but a brief trek," the barrel-chested man said as he prepared to shove off.

"I sense a big wind coming. See the storm clouds and the waves?" Manteo pointed toward the water.

"We will be fine," the captain said abruptly.

Manteo grasped his forearm, a gesture the captain did not seem to appreciate.

"I am in charge here," the Englishman growled, shaking his arm free.

"I fear for your safety," the Indian said. "The birds are acting strangely. That is not a good sign."

"I care nothing for the superstitions of savages," Stafford shot back. "We will go."

"I don't think we should go," Ben whispered anxiously to Lindsey. "Let's see what T.J.—"

But when they turned to their teacher, they saw that he had suddenly fallen asleep.

"Oh no!" Ben's voice held a touch of panic.

Lindsey's eyes widened. "He can't take us back yet!" she cried. "We don't know what happened, and Andrew's too far away to hold on to T.J."

"We'd better get back to shore," Ben urged.

Lindsey looked at her brother, who was staring in alarm at his slumbering teacher. This was the first time since they'd arrived at the Lost Colony that T.J. had suddenly fallen asleep like this. They had to get Andrew.

"Manteo, they must not go," she heard her brother say in an urgent voice.

The Indian shrugged unhappily. "They will not listen. Let us go to our work."

But Andrew wouldn't let it go at that. He raced toward Captain Stafford's boat. "Take me with you!" he begged.

"Go away!" the angry man shouted. "We have enough hands."

"But I must go!" Andrew said. "You don't understand what will happen if I don't."

"Please take him!" Lindsey shouted from their boat as it

began to pitch and toss on the waves.

The captain's rage boiled over, and he cuffed Andrew across the chest with his powerful arm. Andrew went sprawling into the sand.

"Creep!" Lindsey screamed at him.

Before Manteo could help the boy to his feet, both boats were well offshore. Suddenly T.J. awakened, but it was too late to do anything about getting Andrew. Ben quickly told him what had happened.

"Somehow, God will work all of this out for the best," the teacher said. But his voice was shaky.

Twenty minutes later and a third of the way across Croatoan Sound, the wind gusts became even stronger. Rain pelted them, and the rocking swells made rowing difficult. Lindsey clung for dear life to the side of the wooden craft. She wished like everything that Andrew were with them. She hated the thought of his missing the solution to the mystery. Even worse was the possibility that he might not be able to get back home.

"Maybe we should turn back," John Wyles screamed to Stafford across the water that separated them.

"Nay! We will be safer going all the way and seeking shelter," the commander ordered.

The vessels were hurled on the waves like baseballs in the hand of a wild pitcher. Water spilled into the boats, soaking everyone.

"Bail!" Wyles yelled to Lindsey, Ben, and Thomas. He tossed wooden buckets to them, and they scooped water out of the boat while other hands rowed.

Lindsey struggled to stay upright as she bailed. Her

drenched hair kept falling over her eyes, and the wind roared in her ears. A half hour later the battered boats and their crews landed like beached whales on the mainland. Lindsey had been too busy to even be seasick during the ordeal. Now she lay in the sand at the water's edge and offered half her breakfast to the sound. Several others did likewise.

Finally, weak and dizzy from the strain, she lifted her head. She couldn't believe what she saw. Across the sound a tower of water slammed into Roanoke Island!

Chapter Thirteen

For once Captain Stafford didn't know what order to give. Lindsey watched as he stood helplessly, trying to figure out what to do. To her surprise, T.J. took charge. He may not have been a sailor, but he knew a hurricane when he saw one.

"We only have two minutes to get to high ground," he yelled above the wind. "Two minutes!"

His forcefulness seemed to take Captain Stafford by surprise. Obviously, Thomas Wakesnoris knew what he was talking about.

"Pull the boats farther onto the shore!" T.J. directed as rain washed his face. "Hurry, men!"

The wind howled around the men and boys as they hauled the boats in the punishing rain.

"Lindsey!" T.J. grabbed her attention. "Get up that hill over there! It's the highest spot around." He pointed toward a nearby embankment. Tall pines hovered over it, bending wildly in the gale. When she hesitated he screamed, "Run!"

Lindsey ran, and as she did, she found it harder and harder to stay on her feet. Her drenched hair blew against her face, covering her eyes. Her delicate body struggled to stay upright in the mighty wind. She swayed and tottered like a sapling. Then, suddenly, she felt adrenaline surge within her. She made it to the top and positioned herself against a tree trunk, clinging to it for dear life.

Close behind her the men, Ben, and Thomas labored up the incline. They had pulled the boats as far in as they could. Now it was time to save themselves.

"Hurry, men!" T.J. shouted. "Hurry!"

Normally they could have covered the next few yards in a matter of seconds. Not so today. The wind blew against them, snapping and felling trees like pencils at the mercy of an angry school child.

Waves gushed over the beach. They licked the men's heels like dogs in hot pursuit. Lindsey watched as each man who made it to the top of the hill reached down to pull up the guy behind him, while someone else pushed from behind.

"Hurry, man!"

"Push!"

"Do not give up!"

Above the noise they coaxed, encouraged, and sometimes yelled at each other. As the men struggled to safety, the rain burst upon them from the explosive sky.

Father, please help everyone make it to safety, Lindsey prayed. *And please be with Andrew.* For the first time since the adventure had begun, Lindsey felt truly afraid. A sob caught in her throat as she continued, *He's a terrible bother, Lord, but I love him. Don't let him drown in this storm.*

Just then a small tree uprooted from the hurricane-force winds rocketed past her. Lindsey screamed as a leafy branch from the sapling smacked Captain Stafford in the head, and he went down on the embankment. John Wyles and Thomas Archard dragged him with their remaining strength to the top of the hill.

Ben tottered over to Lindsey, and they hugged each other.

Soon the other men crowded around under the bending trees, wondering what to do next.

"We must huddle together!" T.J. shouted above the din of the storm.

"Huddle?" John Wyles questioned the strange word.

"Gather together," T.J. called back. "Keep your heads low!" His voice was growing hoarse. He had one thing more to say, however. "Objects will be hurling like spears from all directions. You must lay low. I strongly suggest that we pray for deliverance!"

"Hear! Hear!" shouted the men in response.

"Let us lift our hearts to God!" John Wyles cried out.

All around Lindsey rose the muffled sounds of men at prayer. Waves leaped over the shore, striking to within a few feet of their perch, as now and then a sob ripped through the train-like roar of the wind. Suddenly Thomas Archard cried out, "Who is this, then, that even the winds and the waves obey him?"

T.J. staggered over to Lindsey and Ben. Rain-drenched, T.J. and Ben hovered so close to her that she felt their sides as they breathed. The small band of colonists clustered together and continued to pray, toughing out the storm for nearly three hours.

Abruptly a great calm settled upon them. Lindsey felt the sun break over her like a precious, golden ointment. The colonists were so encouraged and relieved that they leaped from their squatting positions on the wet ground. She joined them in their joyful dance. In their torn, soggy clothes they encircled each other in enormous hugs of relief.

"Praise the Lord!" they yelled.

"Hallelujah!"

"We are saved!"

Lindsey saw, however, that T.J. was not smiling.

"What is wrong?" Thomas asked him.

"It is too soon for celebration," T.J. said sternly.

Thomas, looking like a wet sheep with his matted curly hair, leaned closer. "Are you also thinking of our fellows on Roanoke Island?" he asked soberly.

T.J. clasped his shoulder. "That, too. But Thomas, this is what is known as the eye of the storm. It is not over yet."

Thomas shook his head. "I am so deeply impressed by your knowledge. How can you know so very much?"

But T.J.'s attention was focused on a conversation a few feet away. Lindsey started listening, too. It seemed that a few of the men, led by Captain Stafford, were talking about heading back to Roanoke Island.

The captain waved others toward the shore and said, "Let us leave this terrible place!"

"Stop!" T.J. hollered.

"What is this?" Stafford asked, his dark eyes blazing at the challenge. He stood before T.J., his hands on his hips.

"The storm is not over," T.J. said.

"Not over?" Stafford sputtered. "Not over! Look, man, at the sun! God has smiled on us."

"Good captain, this will not last. I know these storms."

"Care you not for the poor devils we left behind?"

"More than I can say. I also care for our small company. We will not be of any help to our fellows on the island should we be drowned in our foolish haste to get to them." T.J. spoke hoarsely, but his calm sense of authority spoke loudly.

Lindsey sensed Stafford's irritation. The captain obviously wasn't used to being questioned. He stared defiantly at the tall, slim teacher. "I give you fifteen minutes, good sir. Then if the sun still glows, we return to the Cittie of Raleigh."

T.J. wasn't satisfied. "Captain, it could take thirty minutes to two hours for the storm to return. I beg you to listen to me."

"I am a man of the sea. I, too, know the weather. I give you but fifteen minutes," Stafford said firmly.

"Are we in the eye of the storm?" Lindsey quietly asked T.J. a few moments later.

"That's exactly what it is."

"How long do you think it will last?" Ben asked.

"As I told Captain Stafford, it could be a half hour to two hours. It varies." T.J. grimly pursed his lips.

"What if it still hasn't happened then, and Captain Stafford insists we leave?" Lindsey asked in disbelief. There was no way they could survive on the sound when the deadly winds assaulted them for the second time.

T.J.'s eyes met hers. "We won't go," he said firmly. "We shouldn't have come in the first place."

Now Lindsey was truly worried. She spent the next ten minutes under a tree, her wet skirt fanned around her, trying to pray. In the distance she saw Roanoke Island and wondered what had happened to everyone. Then she crept closer to T.J.

"Are you praying, too?" she asked.

He nodded. "But if you have something on your mind, you may say it," he answered kindly.

"Just before the wind hit us," she began, "I saw a wall smash over Roanoke Island. Was I seeing things?"

"I'm afraid not."

"What was it?"

"Storm surge," he answered simply. "Have you ever heard of it?"

"I've heard it mentioned on the Weather Channel. What is it?"

"It's when a hurricane makes landfall," T.J. explained, sounding very much like the teacher he was. However, he didn't tell her that the storm surge is deadlier if it happens at high tide. This one had. Or that the storm surge kills nine out of ten people who die in hurricanes. But she had heard that, too, on television.

"Maybe that's what happened to the lost colonists, T.J.," she guessed. "Only Andrew's with them now." Her voice caught. "So is Bess, and I owe her an apology for saying something mean to her."

"Shh," he soothed. "God will work everything out for good."

"Now then, good friends!" Captain Stafford's voice rent the stillness. "We must betake ourselves to Roanoke!"

Several men moved toward the beach.

"T.J., do something!" Lindsey whispered frantically, clutching his arm.

He stood and addressed the men, some of whom seemed uncertain. "I implore you to remain behind! The danger will return."

"Who listens to this rot?" the captain challenged. "Return with me at once. We must seek the fate of our fellow colonists."

All but T.J., John Wyles, Lindsey, Ben, and Thomas followed the captain's order.

Stafford went over to John Wyles and poked his nose in

the man's face. "You are a fool, John," Stafford snapped.

"Perhaps," Wyles said calmly. "But here I stay. You will, of course, leave us one of the boats, Captain?"

"Trust me," Stafford replied.

Then the captain led the men down the slippery embankment to the shore.

"Why don't you stop them?" Lindsey cried. "They'll never make it if they leave now!"

"Are you certain of yourself, Thomas?" asked Wyles. He seemed to be having second thoughts.

"Absolutely, John. The winds will return very shortly."

Wyles nodded. "I believe you."

"But what about them?" Lindsey burst into tears.

"Dear child," John Wyles said, clasping her shoulder, "not even God will force a man against his will."

"But they'll die!" she shouted.

Wyles gave T.J. a knowing look over Lindsey's head, as if to assure him she would be all right.

"I am going to walk down to the shore," Thomas said. "I want to see the men off."

"Stay with us here, young man," T.J. ordered. "The winds will return any time now."

"I can always hurry back," Thomas insisted.

"No."

Thomas stayed put. Within the next few minutes T.J. found an even higher spot for them where a huge tree had fallen. Lindsey saw that its large root ball could be used for their protection.

"We must stay close to each other," her teacher said. "The winds will be even worse this second time."

Fifteen minutes after Captain Stafford pulled away from the shore, the eye of the storm winked evilly past them. Huge gusts of winds rampaged against the mainland. Lindsey and her companions pressed against the sides of the root ball and each other. Trees snapped in two above them. The ground shook like an earthquake. All the while the tiny group prayed to God for protection. Lindsey shuddered to think what was happening to the foolish men who had followed Captain Stafford.

They remained in their crouched and praying positions for so long that Lindsey's arms and legs went numb. She lost track of time as the storm shook the foundations of her life.

Strange thoughts pelted her spirit like hailstones. If she died now, would there be no record of her existence in the future? Would it be like her parents had never given birth to her? Would she be Lindsey Wakesnoris of 1587 or Lindsey Skillman of the 1990s? She was completely at God's mercy.

She had a sense now of what it meant to be helpless before God. Dead in sin, humans have only one hope of escape, the death Jesus died to pay for human sin. Lindsey had known all that for years. Still, she always felt she wasn't as bad as most people, that her sins weren't so terrible. Lindsey knew she was smart and looked good. She felt that God must be especially pleased to have her as his child.

But now she lay before him with nothing to praise her. She didn't have any answers to their dilemma. She was in an ugly dress that she'd worn for so many days she'd lost count. She had insulted her friend, Bess. She was wet and chilled to the bone.

Here I am, Lord, she prayed. *I have nothing to offer you but*

*myself, and I don't look all that great right now. I've been self-cen-
tered and petty. Now I'm on the verge of dying. I'd really like to see
my brother again—and my parents and my home.* She swallowed
hard as the crashing rain washed her tears. *But, Lord, I want you
more than anything at all. More than my family or my life in
Williamsburg or my brains or my looks. It's okay with me whatever
you decide to do with me.*

Just then peace flushed Lindsey's spirit of its selfishness
and pride. It was a peace more powerful than the rain that
pounded all around her. Whatever happened, God would
never leave her nor forsake her. And that was enough.

That peace, however, was immediately put to the test when
the storm abated. The sun came out, and the group of be-
draggled, water-logged people staggered about, wringing their
clothes and shaking excess water from their hair. Thomas and
Ben had gone down to the shore to check out the situation. As
Lindsey stood wringing the skirt of her dress, the two boys
came running back up the hill toward them.

"Both boats are gone!" Ben cried.

Chapter Fourteen

Later, in the strangely calm, sunny aftermath of the hurricane Lindsey foraged through their soggy belongings for some food. John Wyles worked patiently nearby trying to start a fire with wet wood, while T.J., Ben, and Thomas collected drinkable water.

"I hope they come up with more than I did," Lindsey told Wyles.

Just then an acceptable blaze began to crackle at their base near the shore.

"Good job!" Lindsey exclaimed, then quickly clapped a hand over her mouth when she saw the expression on Wyles's face. "Uh, excuse me," she said.

"That is all right." He grinned. "So, what did you find, Lindsey?"

She reluctantly handed him a dented metal pan containing a small amount of sorry-looking cornmeal. "I hope this cooks all right." She frowned as if to say, "Just don't hold your breath."

"That is fine," Wyles said. "Just put it over the fire. We all are so hungry, I think we would eat just about anything."

Lindsey, who felt as soggy as the cornmeal, gladly stood next to the hot flames. Maybe her dress would dry out if she stood there a while. Then it occurred to her that this was Bess's dress and that the girl might never wear it again.

Was that how the colonists died, in the hurricane? Did they all drown? Did her brother drown? A sob caught in Lindsey's throat. A gentle wind blew, but she was so chilled inside that it raised goose bumps next to her armada of mosquito bites. Even now she was slapping at the pests to keep them away.

Wyles seemed to sense her mood. "Tomorrow, when we have recovered from the storm, we will find fresh food. Do not worry."

"I am not worried about food. I keep thinking about the others. What happened to them after that wall of water hit the colony? Then I think about Captain Stafford and the men who tried to go back. I'm furious with them for taking both boats. Then I feel guilty because it is likely that all of them died."

Wyles gave her arm a reassuring squeeze. "I know, Lindsey. This has been a most terrible day. Let us imagine that those men did not take both boats and that the water claimed the other."

Lindsey liked that thought. "What will happen now?" she asked. She knew she must be drawing to the end of her Lost Colony adventure.

"The Lord will take care of us," he replied.

The afternoon sped by as Lindsey and her companions tried to dry their clothes and meager food supplies. T.J. had come up with a little more food than Lindsey had found, but not much. At night they spread the few blankets they had on the damp ground. Lindsey didn't feel much like talking. No one did, as if the storm had blown the words right out of everyone's mouths.

T.J. seemed especially quiet. Lindsey also noticed that he

had become pale again. This worried her, of course, but not even her concern or her physical discomfort robbed her of rest. She was so exhausted from the day's ordeal that she fell into a deep sleep.

Lindsey opened her eyes to a sunny morning that bore no resemblance to the previous day's turmoil. She sat up and stretched, gazing at the calm waters of the sound as they lapped the shore.

"It's good to be alive, Lord," she whispered, lifting her face to the gentle breeze. "Please let Andrew be alive, too, and many others on Roanoke Island." She chose to keep hoping for the best.

"Lindsey," a familiar voice said, breaking into her thoughts.

She turned to see T.J. reclining on a wool blanket. His longs legs extended way beyond its length. He looked deathly pale, and his voice was as scratchy as the blanket.

"T.J.!" She jumped up and knelt by his side. "What's wrong?"

He took her hand in his. "I'm just feeling a little weak. I'll be okay."

Lindsey put her hand to his forehead to check his temperature. It was hot.

"How's your leg?"

"I don't know."

"Do you mind if I take a look?"

He shook his head. Lindsey was alarmed to see that blood had seeped through the heavy tan stocking covering T.J.'s calf. She carefully lifted the bottom of his britches in order to remove his sock. The nasty bullet wound wasn't only bleeding—a foul-smelling slime oozed from it.

"It's infected," she whispered, feeling queasy.

"What's that?" T.J. tried to sit up and look, but he was so weak that he fell right back down.

"It's infected. I think the storm set you back."

Lindsey reached into her small leather satchel and withdrew a linen handkerchief. It wasn't exactly clean, but at least she hadn't blown her nose on it. She started wiping away the gunk on her teacher's leg, wishing she had peroxide and Neosporin.

She couldn't let anything happen to T.J. As far as Lindsey knew, getting home depended entirely on his ability to time travel. Fear lashed at the peace God had given her the previous day.

Soon John Wyles, Ben, and Thomas returned from their morning foraging. They had awakened at dawn to go in search of food. They had looked for edible roots and berries, nuts the storm had shaken loose from trees, and fish swimming near the shore. Birds and small animals either had fled to safety and not yet returned or had perished in the hurricane. They carried several fish now and a few varieties of nuts. Not exactly Wheaties and over-ripe bananas, but at least it was food.

When Ben saw T.J.'s leg, he was so shocked that he dropped his fish. Thomas quickly retrieved it from the sand and rinsed it off in the water.

"I knew you were weak, T—uh, Father," Ben stammered, "but I had no idea…" He pointed to the mean-looking sore.

"Master Wyles," Lindsey called, "what do you do for an infection?"

"Infection?" he repeated the unfamiliar word slowly. Then he saw the wound, and his jaw dropped. He dug into his bag and found some kind of ointment, which he smeared on the wound. T.J. moaned; it must have stung.

"What is that?" T.J. asked.

"'Tis a balm used by sailors. It is foul, but effective."

Lindsey didn't eat much. They were stranded, all their colleagues had died in the storm—maybe even Andrew. Now T.J. was gravely ill. Although it was sunny and warm, a storm cloud hovered over Lindsey's spirit.

After breakfast, she sat next to T.J. to keep an eye on him. By now he was slightly delirious. He kept muttering about giving an upcoming test. Lindsey frequently gave him fresh water to sip; she would hold the pewter cup to his cracked lips. "Dear Lord," she prayed continually, "please spare his life."

Her sense of adventure was at an all-time low. Lindsey knew in her heart that unless T.J. recovered, she and the other "Dreamers" would never make it back home. "Lord, I don't mean to be selfish," she prayed, "like I usually am"—she couldn't help but think of Bess—"but I'd really like to go home again." Then she started thanking him for her blessings—life and hope, forgiveness and renewal, family and friends, and if she had to let all these go, heaven.

By late afternoon, Thomas, Ben, and John Wyles had laid up water and food supplies for the night. They had also created a lean-to shelter out of fallen tree branches. Lindsey looked up then from where T.J. restlessly tossed on the blanket and gave a shout.

"Look!" She pointed toward the water.

All of them stopped what they were doing and put their

hands to their foreheads to shade their eyes from the sun. Far in the distance, a dark form appeared on the water. It was coming toward them.

"I believe it is a dugout!" Thomas cried a few minutes later. "There appear to be two people in it."

"I wonder who?" Lindsey yelled.

"What a wonderful sight!" Ben said.

Before many minutes had passed, they saw who it was—Manteo and Andrew! The two made long, deep passes into the water with their hand-hewn paddles. When at last they reached the mainland, they quickly pulled the dugout onto the sand.

"Oh, God, thank you so much," Lindsey breathed.

Andrew was the first one out of the dugout. He ran to his sister and cousin.

"Andrew!" Lindsey and Ben screamed together.

He broke into a huge grin and gladly accepted their bear hugs.

"I thought you guys were dead." Andrew's voice trembled.

"We were afraid for you, too," Lindsey said.

"Manteo!" they shouted then as the Indian came toward them.

Everyone started talking at once. A few minutes later, however, Andrew and Manteo became quiet when Lindsey told them about T.J.'s condition. She took them to the teacher, who folded his hands in prayer and muttered thanks to God for sparing Andrew and Manteo.

The Indian had brought his leather satchel, containing all that was left of his possessions. He drew some herbs from it and mixed them with water. T.J. drank the potion as Manteo applied a gel-like substance to the festering leg wound.

"Is it too late?" Lindsey asked the Indian privately.

"Only if it is God's will," he replied.

Over a meal of fresh crabs and corn bread, Manteo and Andrew told them what had happened when the storm heaved itself upon Roanoke Island.

"Manteo and I were working at the southern part of the island," Andrew explained.

"I was concerned about the weather," his companion added. "There were higher sand dunes there. I knew they would offer protection from high winds and waves."

"Unfortunately, no one believed him," Andrew said quietly. "We tried to get others to come with us, but they refused. They didn't trust Manteo's judgment."

For a moment no one said anything. The only sounds were the sputtering fire and the waves from the sound. Above them the stars shone more brilliantly than Lindsey had ever seen. As Andrew continued, she absently swatted yet another mosquito. She hardly minded, though. Her brother was alive!

"When the storm kicked up, Manteo and I hid on the other side of the highest dune. When it hit, man, did it ever hit!" Andrew fell into modern English as Manteo, Thomas, and John Wyles looked at him quizzically.

Manteo sat still and calm as Andrew told the story of the storm surge.

"I saw this tower of water break over the outer banks nearest us. Then it kept coming. It was like those old movies where the monster gets shot, but he doesn't die."

Lindsey knew her eyes were big, and John, Thomas, and Manteo's expressions said clearly that they didn't understand what movies were. "Whoops!" Andrew said. "There goes my imagination again. Monsters and all that."

"What is a moo-vie?" Thomas Archard frowned as he formed the unfamiliar word.

"It's uh, like a picture that you see in your head," Andrew said clumsily.

"Andrew and I were safe," Manteo said, taking over the telling of the story. "We used the dugout for shelter, leaning it against the dune. When the storm ended, we returned to the fort." He shook his head sadly. "Everyone was gone."

"Everyone?" Lindsey repeated in disbelief. Not Bess, the Dares, Father Martyn…

"There were no survivors."

As the news sank in, Lindsey began to cry softly, as did several others. She had never gotten to apologize to Bess. She looked down at her—Bess's—dress, knowing that no matter how many days she'd worn it, she didn't know if she could take it off now, ever. It was all she had left of her new friend. Oh, how could this have happened? These people had become part of her, and she'd never had the chance to say goodbye.

Manteo explained that several buildings had survived, but the pinnace had disappeared in the storm.

"We carved a message for Governor White," he said, concluding his story. "It says 'Croatoan.' He will know that is where we have gone."

Now she knew what that carved message really meant!

"I will take all of you to Croatoan," Manteo generously offered. "There you will be welcomed as my family."

When the adults and Thomas Archard had fallen asleep that night, Lindsey, Ben, and Andrew walked a short distance from the campsite. They wanted to talk openly by themselves.

"Now that we know what happened to the lost colonists, I wonder if we can go home," Lindsey said, then grinned slightly. "Are you still going to get T.J. fired?" she asked Andrew.

He gave a little laugh. "Not if you guys don't fire me as a brother and a cousin. I've behaved pretty badly."

Soft laughter met his confession. Then they became thoughtful again.

"I wonder if anyone will believe us when we get home," Lindsey reflected.

"Or if they'll know we've been gone at all," Ben added.

"I have a feeling it will be like T.J. said," Lindsey observed. "We'll get back, and it will be like time stood still."

"I wonder if when we leave here, anyone will realize we're gone," Andrew said.

His sister shivered. "That gives me the willies. I mean, to think that you've been somewhere for so long and so much has happened, and you never even left your mark."

"Then again, it has a certain niceness to it," Andrew countered. "I'm glad no one will remember how awful I've been. Besides, maybe we didn't touch other people's lives here, but they sure touched mine."

Lindsey frowned. "I haven't exactly been the nicest person here either. I really insulted Bess." She told them what had happened. "I haven't always been nice to you guys, either. Will you forgive me?"

"Sure," they quickly said together.

"And me, too?" Andrew requested.

Another round of "sures" rose up.

"So, I guess I'm the only perfect one around here," Ben

said, obviously trying to lighten things up. "I've been a good cousin, son, and gentlemen." He puffed his chest.

"We just don't deserve you, Ben!" Lindsey joked.

"I've been wondering if we should tell anyone about this adventure when we get back," Andrew said a few moments later.

"Me, too." Lindsey nodded. "We've solved a centuries-old mystery! Wouldn't it be cool to tell the world that a hurricane wiped out all but two of the colonists, and that they went to Croatoan with Manteo?"

Ben dropped his chin in his palm. "Yeah, but who'll believe us?"

"Our parents?" Andrew suggested.

"I don't think so," Lindsey said slowly. "They might fire T.J. on the spot."

Andrew grinned. "You know, it's funny, but I really like him, after all."

"The thing is, if T.J. sticks around, we may end up time traveling again," Ben warned.

Lindsey laughed. "I wouldn't mind!"

"Well, let's get back first," her cousin pointed out. "And that all depends on T.J., doesn't it?"

Andrew shook his head gently. "I think," he said in a soft tone, "that it's really up to God."

Ben and Lindsey looked at him incredulously. "You've really changed," Ben said.

"I guess so." Andrew nodded. "Let's pray," he said then. "Let's put ourselves and T.J. completely in God's hands. That's what Manteo and I did, and we're here to tell about it."

"He is so nice," Ben said.

"Yes, he is. And he's forgiven me for how badly I treated him when I was with George Howe. All that stuff about poisoning the wells!"

After they prayed, they walked back to the clearing where everyone slept soundly, including T.J.

"Ben, Andrew," Lindsey cried in an excited but hushed tone, "his fever is gone! He's breathing normally."

They leaned closer to check their teacher's condition. Lindsey had her hand on T.J.'s forehead, and the boys each had hold of a wrist to check his pulse, when suddenly they felt a strange numbness creeping up their hands.

"I think it's happening again!" she shouted as a prickly sensation started rushing through her limbs. "Hold on!"

Within seconds—or was it that time really did stop?—they were all back in their classroom on the first floor of their house in Williamsburg. The three students were hanging onto T.J.'s arms, whooping and hollering for joy.

"Wh-what's happening?" T.J. opened his eyes and stared at them in bewilderment.

"You're never going to believe it!" Ben laughed. He went to push up his glasses and discovered that they were back! "No one's going to believe it."

As Lindsey jumped up and down in her excitement, she felt something jingling in her pocket. She reached into it and discovered Governor John White's leather pouch filled with casting counters. With a big smile she tossed it up and caught it.

"Then again..."